OBEYING CHRIST IN A CHANGING WORLD

VOL. 3

The Changing World

In the last quarter of the twentieth century the churches of the western world are facing their biggest challenge yet. Secularism continues to advance. Millions now regard Christianity as a picturesque but superstitious irrelevance. Only a tiny percentage of the population goes to church regularly. The future prospects look bleak.

Yet much goodwill remains, as the response to the Archbishops' 'Call to the Nation' revealed. And there are signs of spiritual renewal in the churches. One of these is the remarkable post-war resurgence of evangelicals in the Church of England. They emphasize the supreme lordship of Jesus Christ in every department of life, the authority of the Bible, and the supernatural power of Christ to change people.

The second National Evangelical Anglican Congress (Nottingham 77) is entitled 'Obeying Christ in a Changing World'. This book is the third of three volumes which introduce its theme. It asks probing questions about the changing world in which we live. How are Christians to relate to the way in which power is exercised in our democracy? What is the effect of the power of the media? How should laws be made, and how can a Christian evaluate them? How should Christians respond to the issues of race, sex and the distribution of resources?

The aim of this book is not to give slick answers, but to grapple honestly with contemporary issues in the light of the Bible.

OBEYING CHRIST IN A CHANGING WORLD

General Editor – John Stott

VOLUME I: THE LORD CHRIST
edited by John Stott

VOLUME II: THE PEOPLE OF GOD
edited by Ian Cundy

VOLUME III: THE CHANGING WORLD
edited by Bruce Kaye

OBEYING CHRIST IN A CHANGING WORLD

VOLUME 3

The Changing World

edited by Bruce Kaye

Collins + World
FOUNTAIN BOOKS

First published in 1977 by Fountain Books
and Collins + World

Made and printed in Great Britain
by William Collins Sons & Co. Ltd. Glasgow

CONTENTS

GENERAL INTRODUCTION

The first National Evangelical Anglican Congress was held at Keele University in April 1967. The second is due to take place at Nottingham University in April 1977, and this book is one of its three preparatory documents. Under the overall title 'Obeying Christ in a Changing World' they investigate 'The Lord Christ', 'The People of God' who are committed to his obedience and 'The Changing World' in which they are called to obey him. Although related to a particular Congress, we believe they have more than a transient value and will be of interest to a much wider group than the Congress participants.

Behind each chapter lies the work of a 'research group' which met with the author to stimulate his thinking. The authors are grateful for the help they received from these groups. Yet each author is responsible for his own chapter, and no chapter bears any imprimatur from its group or from the Congress. Further, all the authors have been conscious of the restrictions imposed upon them by the limited space at their disposal.

The mood of these books is, we hope, a reflection of authentic evangelical Christianity. This is an unusual combination of the conservative and the radical, the dogmatic and the agnostic, the fixed and the free. Our starting point is Scripture, which we accept as God's unique and trustworthy revelation. Yet in seeking with loyalty to conserve this truth from God, we attribute no infallibility to our own evangelical traditions. We desire rather to re-examine them radically, that is to say, with a thoroughness which digs down even to their roots. If we seem to the reader to be always sure about the truthfulness of Scripture but sometimes less than sure in our understanding of how to apply it to complex contemporary questions, then he has accurately grasped our mood.

Each chapter is followed by questions to encourage discussion. We hope that our readers will seek to study, as our authors have sought to write, in a spirit of humble and open-minded submission to the authority of God's Word.

John Stott

INTRODUCTION

The authors who have contributed to this book have been subjected to more than the usual amount of stress and criticism in the work they have done. This is because they have belonged to small research groups who met to discuss the areas covered by the chapters, and then later draft versions of the chapters. This process has enriched and sharpened the contribution of the author of each chapter.

There are two points, however, which ought to be remembered about the chapters of this book, since they mark it out from a lot of Christian discussion of the same area of social responsibility, and especially from other contributions by evangelicals. On the one hand, these essays represent an English follow-on from the impetus of the Lausanne Congress on World Evangelization and from the earlier National Evangelical Anglican Congress at Keele in 1967. This impetus has thrust upon evangelicals the challenge of the social commitment of Christians, and it has also placed before them the need to work out how their evangelical tradition interprets and understands in theological terms that commitment. On the other hand, the essays in this volume represent a very particular theological method which will seem a bit strange to some evangelicals.

THEOLOGICAL METHOD

Traditionally, evangelicals have done their theology by trying to work out the basic principles from the Scriptures and then by either applying these scriptural principles to the question under discussion or seeking to discover their practical implications. We might call this a deductive approach to doing theology. The method which has been adopted in this volume runs in the opposite direction, without, however, denying the propriety or necessity of the older method. Here an issue in the present situation has been taken, and then analysed in depth to see what is at stake in it and how Christian truth may be related to it. We might call this an inductive approach to doing theology.

The whole question of theological method was discussed at some length very early in the preparatory stages of planning for Nottingham 77. The group concerned with the social responsibility section advocated the fairly thorough going use of the inductive approach, and further argued that particular topics should be selected from the various areas to be covered, and that these topics should be studied in depth. This principle of selection would, it was hoped, help us to avoid treating broad issues in a superficial way. It in no way represents a commitment to what some Liberation Theologians call 'a new way of doing theology', though it does indicate a wholehearted acceptance of the place of 'critical reflection on praxis' in the total theological exercise. The method of the first volume of these three books *The Lord Christ* reflects a different theological method. That is because its authors are seeking to deal with different kinds of questions. It also includes a full discussion of this very matter of the use and interpretation of the Bible.

It should not be thought that this opening up of the issue of theological method by evangelicals implies any diminution of our commitment to the authority of the Scriptures. However, it does mean a recognition of some of the dangers of the older text-book, deductive method when that is the only method used. This older method often had three serious shortcomings. In the first place, it treated the Scriptures as if they had the overall literary character of a single law-code, and ignored the situational and cultural factors which conditioned each distinct piece of biblical teaching. This often made for a shallow understanding of Scripture. Secondly, it often overlooked the need to understand clearly the social and cultural factors which shape the present situation to which the biblical truth is being applied. Thirdly, those using this method have often been so completely attached to the thought of Scripture as divine truth, and therefore of its absolute and universal authority, that it was difficult for them to enter into effective dialogue with those who paid more attention to the human and circumstantial character of Scripture. This has frequently caused suspicion and misunderstanding. What we assert here is that the method adopted throughout these volumes, and in particular in this third volume, is more scriptural and not less.

In dealing with questions of social responsibility, as we are in this book, there were a number of reasons for adopting the more inductive approach. In the first place, it is particularly appropriate when looking at specific issues of social ethics. For then the full complexities of the present circumstances are properly and adequately taken into consideration. Secondly, it best suited the membership of the research groups which worked with the authors. These groups were made up of lawyers, doctors, politicians and academics in the social sciences. One may illustrate this point by reference to chapter 2, The Power of the Media, which is as close to a completely group production as anything could be, and with which all the members of the group wish to be associated. Though the experience of the author is that of an educationist and academic, the group was composed of people who are themselves deeply involved in the media. A third reason for using the more inductive approach was that it seemed to be an appropriate contribution to the developing theological awareness and activity of evangelicals. To include in the preparatory material for a National Evangelical Anglican Congress a complete volume which is so fully committed to this method is an attempt to show that, rightly used, it has a legitimate place in true and authentic evangelicalism.

There are certain characteristics of this method which should be clearly understood. The contributors to this book, and the people who have worked with them, have taken a particular issue of contemporary significance as their starting point. They have then attempted to analyse the circumstances and facts of that issue in order to identify what principles and values are at stake. Next, since some things are more important than others, they have drawn what might be called an 'importance profile', because only when priorities have been clarified can guidelines for action be established. What is sought here is a *Realpolitik* and a *Realethik* which arise from the concrete circumstances and problems which Christians face in today's changing world and which faithfully express the gospel by which Christians seek to live in that world.

EVANGELICALS AND SOCIAL RESPONSIBILITY

This leads to the second point which is noteworthy about the essays in this volume. They are part of a new and welcome thrust in modern evangelicalism, namely towards a fuller commitment to, and better understanding of, the Christian's social responsibility, especially at the institutional and political level. It is true, of course, that evangelicals can look back to an honourable record of social concern in the nineteenth century in such areas as the abolition of slavery. During this century, however, we have not been in the forefront of social endeavour, to say the least. Then the 1967 Keele Congress issued two significant signals: first that evangelical Anglicans were now going to commit themselves more fully to the life of the Church of England, and secondly that they recognized a clear commitment to work out their faith in the world in which they live. In the late sixties a few books were published by such people as Sir Norman Anderson and A. N. Triton, but it was not until the seventies that evangelicals began to get down to work on their commitment. During this period a number of groups were formed, including the Evangelical Race Relations Group, the Shaftesbury Project and the Grove Ethics Group, each working in different ways in this area.

In 1974 the Lausanne Congress on World Evangelization gave fresh impetus to these efforts. It also added a new dimension to the debate by linking Christian social responsibility to evangelism. A considerable amount of ecumenical and liberation theology had virtually identified these two, and Lausanne was at pains to distinguish them. Clause 5 of the Lausanne Covenant on social responsibility was placed immediately after that on the nature of evangelism. It captures the new emphasis so well that it is worth quoting in full.

> We affirm that God is both the Creator and the Judge of all men. We therefore should share his concern for justice and reconciliation throughout human society and for the liberation of men from every kind of oppression. Because mankind is made in the image of God, every person, regardless of race, religion, colour, culture, class, sex or age, has an intrinsic dignity because of which he should be respected and served, not exploited. Here too we express penitence both for our neglect and for having sometimes regarded evangelism and social concern as mutually exclusive. Although reconciliation with man is not reconciliation with God, nor is social action evangelism, nor is political liberation salvation, nevertheless we affirm that evangelism and socio-political involvement are both part of our Christian duty. For both are necessary expressions of our doctrines of God and man, our love for our neighbour and our obedience to Jesus Christ. The message of salvation implies also a message of judgement upon every form of alienation, oppression and discrimination, and we should not be afraid to denounce evil and injustice wherever they exist. When people receive Christ they are born again into his kingdom and must seek not only to exhibit but also to spread its righteousness in the midst of an unrighteous world. The salvation we claim should be transforming us in the totality of our personal and social responsibilities. Faith without works is dead.

The post-Lausanne thrust has continued in Britain, as it has elsewhere in the world. In Britain the writings of John Stott have particularly sought to build on and develop the commitments of Lausanne. In London the Islington Conference was devoted to this subject in 1975, and in 1976 a Fellowship of European Evangelical Theologians was formed in the consciousness that it looked back to Lausanne for its origins. The large place given to the consideration of social responsibility at Nottingham 77 is a further sign of the same development.

It should not be thought, however, that anything like an agreed evangelical line on these issues has emerged. All those involved in the production of this book have been feeling their way. The chapters that are presented here are first steps in a long and difficult journey. In taking those steps we have learned to rely upon each other's experience and skills. Indeed, one of the more important by-products of our task has been the extensive involvement of Christians with a wide range of professional competence and experience in the united pursuit of Christian understanding. This is far from a clerical production, and the theologians involved learned to submit to the knowledge of their fellow Christians from other disciplines.

GROUNDS FOR SOCIAL INVOLVEMENT

Two other questions which have been much in our minds, but which have not been discussed in their own right in the chapters that follow, are the basis for our socio-political involvement, and the principles upon which we should direct that involvement. These foundational theological questions have been widely debated by evangelicals; indeed some of the contributors to this volume have written on them elsewhere. There is also a long tradition of Christian thinking about them. At least three different foci can be identified in the discussion of the basis of our social involvement. Some simply appeal to the commandment to love the neighbour. This is the second great commandment which Jesus gave to his disciples, and it should be held by Christians together with the great commission to evangelize. This approach has the merit of reflecting the clear and emphatic position of the great commandment in the New Testament, and it gives to the neighbour who is the object of the Christian's love a dignity and integrity which seem to diminish if social involvement is thought of merely as a kind of pre-evangelism.

Others emphasize the idea of Christian calling. Reminiscent of the Reformed tradition, this stresses that the Christian is to fulfil his place in the world as a calling from God. Thus each Christian has a vocation in the world, and because he has received it from God he is to pursue it as unto God. On this understanding the Christian is able to see his role in the structures of society in directly Christian terms.

A third position sees the issue in relation to the lordship of God in the world. This is sometimes seen in terms of creation, and sometimes in terms of the kingdom. Thus the world belongs to God because he created it, and since he created it there is a basic and 'natural' way in which it was designed to function. While this may look at first sight like a return to a form of 'laws of nature', it is in fact quite distinct in that the natural laws in this position are derived not from the observation of the world around us, but from the study of Scripture. Where the kingdom is the focus, the emphasis tends to be on the hope of Christ's return and the establishment of his kingdom. The kingdom has come, in part, with Jesus's life, death and resurrection. Therefore the Christian is involved in living according to the kingdom Christ has introduced and in working towards the kingdom which Christ will establish when he returns.

While it is possible to distinguish between these different grounds for social involvement, it is not possible to separate them. The quotation of Clause 5 of the Lausanne Covenant above is a good example of how they interlock, and other examples will appear in this book. Questions that arise particularly under the creation heading include: What is the nature of the state, and what are its responsibilities? What is justice in a pluralistic society? In what sense are men to be thought of as 'made in the image of God'? Are there such things as 'creation orders', and is marriage one of them? It will be clear that these are the issues which specially underlie the chapters of this book.

You will not find in this volume a set of ready-made answers. What you will find is evangelical discussion of current issues. It must be recognized that it is not a purely human enterprise in which we are engaged. God is the Lord who reveals his truth and purpose to those who seek them, and though we shall certainly be given some light, enough to live by, we cannot guarantee that either now or later we shall be given answers that are either simple or final. Rather we should hope and pray that through working together in humility we may come to know more of God's presence, purpose and work in his world and among his people, so that we may speak God's life-giving word in the perplexities of the present human situation with integrity, relevance and humility. More than this is not for us to ask.

BRUCE KAYE

I

Power in our Democracy

JOHN GLADWIN
Tutor at St John's College Durham

One of the encouraging features of modern evangelicalism is its growing concern in the field of politics. There seems to be an increasing awareness that Christian belief has something radical and creative to say to all who are seeking for right values, attitudes, and policies in the shaping of our community life. The context of such a life is the world which God has made, and mankind whom he has redeemed in his Son Jesus Christ. We know that God has met us within our history, that we can know his character and person through his work, that he has met with us personally in the real man his Son Jesus Christ, that his love embraces all his creation, and his purposes encompass every part of our life and experience. To know all this is to enter into a new world and a new way of living. Such a commitment, to live for God our Creator and Redeemer in his world, affects every one of our relationships from the most intimate to the most political. Family and community, neighbour and world, are under the challenge of discipleship.

This revived concern in evangelicalism is only one aspect of a generally renewed awareness in the Church of England of the importance of proper theological reflection upon our contemporary social and political decision-making. In the period immediately after 1945 the Church let slip many of the initiatives which had been taken in the middle years of the twentieth century. William Temple and others had set the pace in seeking to think through what shape and form society ought to take for the last part of the twentieth century. The momentum of this debate was lost, however, as the Church tied itself up in matters of internal reform: Canon Law, Liturgy, Synods, Union schemes etc. With many of these concerns now out of the way, there is evidence of strong moves by the Church to give more time and weight to the social aspects of our Christian mission. The work of the General Synod's Board of Social Responsibility plays a central part in stirring the embers. The task is a vital one. There is a prophetic ministry to fulfil as a fundamental part of our mission and our testimony to Jesus.

The Church, however, must exercise care as it returns to this field. There is neither room nor welcome for any triumphalist re-entry. We must avoid giving the impression that we have all the answers sewn-up or that we have a clear strategy for setting our world to rights. The involvement of the whole Church in the contemporary debate about structures and values in the social order must evidence the marks of Christian humility. We are called to listen with sympathy to the full range of the contemporary debate, to question and to probe, to seek after the right Christian values and to begin to understand their practical significance. This discussion must be conducted in such a way that the eventual stance taken by the institutional Church develops as much from the experience of the Christian man on the assembly line, in the classroom, in management, in the social services, in the County Hall, as it does from the academic and ecclesiastical world. The experience of those who are already deeply engaged in mission within the sensitive areas of our social order must not only be consulted but also must share in directing the nature of the debate and of policy formulation.

This paper is a result of reflection upon discussion which took place between people involved in different levels of political life and those involved in theological work and pastoral ministry. The discussion uncovered some deep differences of opinion as it sought to lay bare the basic problems with which we all contend. It also uncovered a deeply held common concern for the unique problems our society faces – the problems of coping democratically with decline. The required economic stringency and political discipline have helped in clarifying the fundamental choices of value which are before us. The paper presented here is, therefore, but a contribution to a debate which must go on if we are to be obedient to Christ in our society today.

LIVING WITH CHANGE

There is no Christian blue-print for social order, political institutions, or economic structures. Christianity is a revealed and a historical religion. God has unfolded his purposes within the on-going experience of human endeavour and history. Change and development are an integral part of our life. Our history evidences periods of relative stability and periods of rapid change. To seek to stay in the same place, to fossilize procedures, is to invite the on-going experience of human history to pass us by, leaving us in the back-waters. Christians are committed to a dynamic attitude to experience. As pilgrims and travellers we are called to experiment by faith. We witness both the decay of the old order and the developing life of the Kingdom of God. We expect the institutions of our life to change and we expect to be part of a changing world. Christians will undoubtedly disagree as to whether they are to initiate change or react to change. We shall disagree as to whether we have a duty to promote a new and better social order or whether we continue to adjust our present order in the light of our experience. Are we revolutionaries or reformers? What our faith does not permit is to be uncritically wedded to the past. We have to live for Christ in a world of change. Our choice for revolution or for reform will depend in part on our principles, and in part on our assessment of the present situation. Some Christians in the modern world call us to give political and social witness to the distinctive values of the Kingdom of God as we see this in Jesus calling us to be active in pursuit of a better society. Other Christians who see the political tasks as an exercise in power in maintaining social order in a fallen world are more concerned for adjusting our institutions in the face of present experience so that good order may continue to be held. Does the Kingdom of God give to us such hope for the future that it directs our political concerns here and now? In contrast, has the politician a duty in the present in maintaining justice for all – a role to be clearly distinguished from the work and life-style of the Kingdom of God?

Moreover, Christians are not agreed in their assessment of the situation. Some are growing in scepticism about the achievements of parliamentary democracy, others are deeply critical of capitalism and growth economics and have grown disillusioned with aspects of the welfare state. This developing pessimism often comes from experience of working in situations of deprivation in housing, education and the social services. It appears that our institutions are frequently unable to come to terms with the most needy groups of people today. Other Christians are more positive in their attitude to present political and economic institutions. They value a Parliamentary democracy, especially when seen in contrast to its alternatives in our world today. They see value in the mixed economies of Western Europe, accepting them as a rough but fairly effective way of preserving the demands of justice and of freedom. They value the welfare state, despite its difficulties, as having done much to promote stability in the modern era.

It will not escape notice that Christians with a pessimistic and radical view of the present need have a habit of picking up radical theologies of the Kingdom, whilst those of a more conservative and optimistic attitude opt for the theologies of creation and of order. The debate, therefore, highlights the problem concerning the way a Christian does his thinking in relation to his situation. How are we to hold together the demands of the situation and the perspectives of the Word of God?

PROBLEMS WITH DEMOCRACY

There has been a lot of debate about the inadequacy of our democratic institutions to cope with the pressures of the last part of this century. There has been talk about the declining power of Parliament and of the Executive at Westminster

There has been demand for more devolvement of power to the regions and to the various institutions which represent different areas of our national life. No doubt some of this talk is misguided in principle and mythological in fact. Yet our institutions do face a severe problem – how to maintain the reality of democracy with order in a situation of decline in the nation's power and wealth. How can those who govern do so with the real consent of the people when there is a need for more stringent economic discipline? Our growing commitment to different forms of political democracy has wide sympathy among Christian people. There has been a long history in our own nation of Christian commitment to constitutional restraints upon the activity of government. The Reformation in England took place within the context of the growth of the power of Parliament. The Puritan movement did much to promote the sense of the need for limits to power, and for rulers to be subject to the call of constitutional justice. Our modern political arrangements provide for protest and the removal of bad government without the need for civil disorder. The reason for our Christian commitment to limits in government power is the tradition within Scripture which opposes claims to absolute power in political institutions. The prophetic distaste for kingship in the Old Testament is due in large part to the fear of what kings will do to the nation (1 Sam. 8:7–9). The Word of God is implacably set against the absolute claims of Pharaoh, of the Assyrians, the Babylonians and the Persians. The attempt by men to assume the absolute to themselves is an affront to God because power in society comes from him. In the New Testament Paul is happy with the Roman government whilst it continues to exercise its God-given office of maintaining law and order with justice. The New Testament becomes opposed to that same system when it arrogates to itself divine roles and opposes the Church of Christ (the Revelation of John). Democracy is a modern way of maintaining some popular control over government.

Yet, because democracy is based upon the notion of popular consent it requires a fair measure of stability. In our social order it is necessary for our institutions to represent the balance of interest between the different economic and social groups which make up its whole life. We are of necessity a plural society, made up of people from different economic classes, from different religions and cultural groups. It is important that all groups are able to see themselves identified with the political institutions of the nation. This is the central problem of the present situation in Northern Ireland. The simple procedures of democracy favour the Protestant argument for majority rule. The spirit of our democracy requires that the minority feel able to identify with the institutions which govern. Therefore, there can only be a settlement which carries the consent of both communities. Northern Ireland in many respects represents the problem of our institutions writ large.

The complexities of a mass population plural society have led to two things happening in relation to each other. The power and status of the politician have declined whilst those of the specialist and expert have grown. At the same time there has been a commitment to educating this generation for participation through critical involvement. People want a greater say, and yet are apathetic in the face of contemporary politics. Thus there has been a tendency for people to get involved in action groups which operate outside the traditional political structure – Oxfam, Shelter, housing groups, anti-abortionist movements, etc. The desire to do something, frustrated at the apparent weakness of the politician in the face of modern bureaucracy, has taken expression elsewhere. People have a growing sense of alienation from a bureaucracy dominated by experts and a sense of frustration in the face of the weakness of political institutions. At the same time the gloom is deepened by the very real possibility that the range of choices before the politician is growing narrower as our wealth and power continue to decline.

Our greatest need today is to re-establish the politician in his proper place in our society. Democracy must be so extended that the politician has direct communication with the community initiating, and forwarding its choices of priority. The skilled expert, who has been trained as the servant of the community, must be brought back from the point of power in decision-making to be the executive servant of the expressed policies of the community. Only the politician as the person who is directly responsible to the democratic process can have the power of government. The people who operate the system – the civil servants and trained experts – must be seen to be responsible to the community by acting responsibly to the community's elected representatives. Nothing is designed more to create alienation and apathy in the community than the sense that the democratic process is a charade and that real power lies with the people who operate the system behind the scenes. To take only the two examples of Town Planning and motorways. Town Planning in the past has often been done from the ivory towers of University Departments without any serious involvement of the people who will have to live with their decisions. In the second case, Governments must not be allowed to run motorways behind people's back doors without those communities being involved, as of necessity, at all levels of decision making. The local community must have an effective say in the way its community life develops and grows.

In our large-scale society, which is essentially plural in texture, grassroots democracy is vital to community stability and order. The people must sense that their elected political representatives have effective power or influence for them. If the choice is to be between tidyness of operation on the one hand and real democracy through community direction on the other, then the balance will have to fall for democracy. Nothing threatens our society so much as a sense of alienation from the points of power. We already see communities in which law and order is collapsing, welfare services barely operating, schools fighting a losing battle against disinterest and downright hostility by both parents and children. What has happened in Northern Ireland in the 'no-go' areas could easily happen in any community which feels aggrieved and alienated from the centre of power in the nation and in local government. Just as the Church is waking up to the need for 'indigenous' Church life and leadership in our communities, so there must be a return of real power to the indigenous leadership of the local community. The drift of the post-war years has been in the direction of the centre and away from the grass roots. It can be seen at all sorts of levels. Labour members of Parliament are less likely today to come from genuinely working class backgrounds and experience. In the 1951 Parliament forty per cent of Labour MP's were from the working class. In 1970 that proportion had dropped to less than twenty-eight per cent. There had been a marked increase by contrast in candidates from the professions.[1] This is not to suggest that present members of Parliament do not do their work well. It is simply to flash a warning light concerning the places of decision-making.

Christians will be deeply concerned over questions of social stability. If this requires some adjustment and development of our procedures to give government greater freedom through greater democratic control then the biblical tradition encourages us to take that road. The Bible is positive in its attitude to government. It looks for and welcomes government which provides for the first needs of the whole community; for the widow, the stranger and the poor. It expects Christian people to be regular in prayer for those who rule, and to be law-abiding citizens. If, in our situation, social cohesiveness and a sense of justice can be furthered by a spread of democratic procedures through all levels of the life of the community then Christians ought to be in the forefront of promoting such a development. Good institutions, with which people identify, are a bulwark against social chaos. Our history over the past few centuries has been a history of extended liberties; the removal of civil disabilities, the extension of the franchise, the growth of the power of the elected House in Parliament. There is little reason to suggest that this development has reached its peak. People today are educated for a critical involvement rather than for passive obedience. The political institutions of the community's life must adapt to meet that growing situation of a desire for participation. The demand for devolution of power to the regions, to the local community, to the factory floor and to the local political party, must be met and given acceptable institutional form.

Such a development is even more important when considered in the light of the growth of international power. If at some levels power is being removed even from the nation/state to bigger institutions, then it becomes vital for the health of the body politic that it drives its roots deep into the heart of the community's life. If, increasingly, we will have to bow to decisions taken in Brussels or at conferences like that on the Law of the Sea, then we must protect our varied and plural social order from the growing possibility of alienation and frustration at the declining power of the individual and of the small group.

The Church will have a double concern in this change. It will be deeply concerned to build procedures of real accountability into politics and it will be concerned to preserve a good and just social order. Both principles, accountability in power and justice in its exercise, have the consistent support of Scripture. Their visible outworking today through a growing concern to extend democracy will arise out of a careful and sympathetic understanding of the present crisis in our political life.

THE CRISIS IN INDUSTRIAL AND ECONOMIC LIFE

Again, in considering this area, we find that Christian people are deeply divided in their assessment of the need and of policy. There are many Christians, particularly in the Western World, who see virtue and value in the freedom which the capitalist system, based on the freedom of private capital, helps to preserve. There are many other Christians, particularly in the Third World, who seek a socialist alternative because of the evidence of injustice and deprivation which are the apparent results of the unfettered operations of private capital. Some Christians will wish to argue the matter in terms of principle for and against capitalism and socialism. Some will wish to argue pragmatically in terms of the economic and social effects of the different systems. Once again, there will be a distinction between those who believe that the system as it stands is capable of reform and adjustment to meet criticism, and those who believe that the system itself is the cause of the problems. For many the debate is concerned with striking a right balance between the call of freedom and the demand of justice. On the side of freedom there is the legitimate fear of power – of any lack of proper checks upon government activity. On the side of justice there is the demand for a better system of distribution of wealth, for a proper recognition of the dignity of work, and for the destruction of some of the unacceptable features of class division.

The problem may be considered in four areas. First, then, the questions of power and of justice. The inheritance of industrialization has given vast economic power to the Western World. A combination of levels of investment, sophistication in technology and the deployment of resources has given power and wealth to the few. There appears to be a vicious circle in deprivation both of wealth and power. With few exceptions the majority in the Third World has to accept the economic terms offered to them by the minority in the developed world of the West. A minority of the world's people commands decision power over the majority of the world's wealth, and consumes the majority of the world's resources. This feature of imbalance embraces the Soviet-controlled part of the world almost as much as the free West. Part of the accumulated wealth is used to create military strength which in turn serves to underline economic and political dominance. The question which is being asked is, 'Are economic systems committed to growth and to wealth contributing to the continued poverty and subservience of the Third World?' The reality of imbalance presses upon nations questions to do with the aims of their economic policies as well as questions to do with the means employed. Is the aim of increased growth and national wealth valid in the light of our experience? Are the means, large-scale private corporations or centralized socialist control, acceptable?

Secondly, the effects of the economic system are not wholly beneficial to society. The way in which industrialization has developed in a capitalist society has led to class division and to conflict of interests. The balance between the interests of capital, of management and of labour have not been easy to maintain. Despite the growing effectiveness of political and industrial organizations which represent the interests of industrial labour it is still true that at almost every level in the material aspects of life, wages, social services, housing, education, health, pension security, labour has the worst part of the deal. Working people have different commitments in industry from both management and capital. In large-scale industry in particular there is little sense of commitment to the firm and little love of the job. The work is often unpleasant and hazardous; its only virtue is that it yields a wage. The prospects in front of working people are not always good. There is not only the threat of unemployment, there is also the threat of decreasing productiveness through age and declining physical fitness. By contrast, management calls for the exercise of trained skills carrying certain rewards in themselves. There are better prospects of promotion based on increasing experience and ability. Even if redundancy is a threat to management, it is less of a threat and the provisions for redundant management are better, as are pension arrangements. For the owners of capital, there is the goal of profit, and with profit, growth, and with growth increased wealth. Our twentieth-century experience suggests that the simple procedures of nationalization do little to remove this basic tension between rival interest groups. Simply to replace private capital with government control changes little. The question of economic structure involves more than questions about ownership of capital. It involves questions about the direction of capital, the control of management, the common participation of workers, manager and owner in the shaping of policy and the right use of resources. It further involves the wider community in questions of the purpose of industry within the bounds of agreed social and political objectives.

Thirdly, our inheritance is one of commitment to growth and to increasing wealth. The free market system is aimed at the consumer. It has the essentially materialistic aim of increasing wealth and of growth in consumption.[2] Modern business has sought to persuade the community that it has need of its products – advertising is frequently geared to encouraging people to spend money in ways which they would not otherwise do. The effect has been to encourage a competitive form of society which some claim is the root of an unhealthy acquisitiveness in society. We have seen that wealth so gained is often gained at the expense of others. Industry has been geared more and more to satisfying the growing demand of the consumer society. Our industry is in no way directed at producing the goods which will help to meet the basic needs of a poverty-stricken world. It produces the gadgets and candy-floss demanded by a community which has been fed on a diet of materialistic excesses. There must be something fundamentally wrong when three quarters of the world would gladly lay hands on what the other quarter put in their dustbins. Christian people have got to give practical witness to the word of Christ that a man's wealth does not consist in the abundance of his possessions. The whole prophetic tradition – so very explicit in Amos – which denounces excess in wealth gained whilst others languish in forms of poverty which result from the abuse of power by the rich has surely more than an echo in our modern age. Growing wealth of this nature cannot be an acceptable objective. Wealth must be the servant not the master of men. If this is the case, then we are inevitably involved in a searching critical analysis of the present economic structures which have contributed to this state of affairs.[3]

Fourthly, our contemporary experience has been one of the growth of economic power in the hands of the few. Industrialization, made to be more sophisticated by developing technology, has led to the growth of large business corporations. It appears that the big multi-national corporations carry real political power in the world through their control of capital. Is this acceptable? Should the representative politician who carries the office of government have to be subject to the power of big business? If in a country of the economic size of Great Britain it is necessary for the Prime Minister to negotiate with the board of Chrysler Motors because of the social damage that might be done by their American-based decisions, how much more must be the power of such companies over the developing nations of the world? It would seem to be virtually impossible for the other interests which make up the life of the corporation to have an effective voice in its policy making. Labour, management *and* the community at large can only react to decisions taken elsewhere. The corporation has the power to deal with opposition in one place by removing its operations to another situation. Many of the problems relate to questions of size. In some cases the effective breaking-up of the concern into smaller units is desirable. We can learn from the experience related in E. F. Schumacher's book *Small is Beautiful*. We can learn from the industrial experiments of Volvo.[4] Yet when all that is said and done we may well find that we still have to deal with a large range of major corporations which just are not amenable to those types of reforms. At present such corporations suffer from all the problems of alienation. There is no great love for Fords at Dagenham, nor for the National Coal Board in Yorkshire. The sense of alienation from the company leads to bad work rates, to industrial strife and to social conflict. The questions which arise here concern the direction of management. Greater democracy must function effectively at all levels. There must be an effective partnership in policy making and policy execution between the political powers, capital and labour. The politician, on behalf of the community, must have an effective voice in leading in developing industrial priorities. Within business life, the work-force, management and capital, must co-operate in developing choices for the community, and in executing agreed objectives in industrial development. All this suggests that we need to think through structures for greater industrial democracy within the large-scale corporations. Once again, this shift in the balance of power must lead to the restoration of the place and power of the politician in our national life. It must also mean a readiness to devolve power to the factory unit, to the small community. In both cases, increase in political power must always go hand in hand with an increased acceptance of the responsibilities of power. A shift towards greater democracy must never be made to mean an emasculation of power and a decreasing ability to make decisions. The purpose in shifting power is to allow the whole community to identify man readily with power in decision-making. Only such a shift can help to overcome the present sense of alienation and frustration within large sections of our community life.

The Marxist political philosophy is directed at the problem of alienation. Wrong economic structures and relationships cause alienation. The way a man relates to the means of production affects not only his environment but the man himself. A privately owned, profit seeking, labour hiring system is bound to lead to alienation. By giving the ownership of the means of production back to the workers, and by making production serve the aims of the whole community, a new situation is created in which alienation is removed. The Marxist has certainly understood the way in which the psychology of the system is an important factor. The way people feel able to identify does affect their work and their sense of responsibility. The Christian believes that God made man a living person in his own image and that man has forfeited some of the privileges of his creation through disobedience and the destruction of the environment of trust. This adds a different dimension to any discussion of alienation. An understanding of creation offers the high aim to man of being able to see his work as opportunity in the exercise of responsible and creative power in obedient fellowship with his creator. That people experience frustration and alienation is due to the failure of man to live in this context of trust in God and personal commitment to the needs of his neighbours. The way people think about themselves and their work is fundamental. The economic system will reflect bad thinking and will encourage it. With the Marxist the Christian will be concerned for the way in which the structures help or hinder in developing a sense of personal commitment and responsibility in people. Christians will also be concerned to bring people to that understanding of man which gives to him individual and personal integrity and offers him a world of trust and responsibility. A purely materialistic philosophy has no hope of achieving this.

Bad structures are a hindrance to godliness of life. They encourage bad attitudes and unacceptable forms of behaviour. They place harsh moral choices before the individual. Bad political structures are an incitement to civil unrest and to an increasing disrespect for the law. How, for example, is the Christian living in the 'no-go' area in Northern Ireland to fulfil his obligation to the civil power? How is he to view his duty in the light of the Apostle's teaching in Romans 13? His problem is the creation of the unhealthy and imbalanced political scene in which he lives. Similarly, bad economic and business structures create serious difficulties of choice for the Christian worker. What is he to do when everyone around him works at half-pace and expects the same of him? What is to be his attitude to clocking-in his mates before they have actually arrived? Structures which encourage deceit and lack of commitment place heavy burdens on his shoulders. The Church has a duty to its members to address itself to the root problems in our institutions which hinder the mature development of human life in 'righteousness of living'. Even if the Church is not in a position to advocate a particular political programme, it is in the position as the trustee of the Word of God, to continually remind the institutions of government of their responsibilities in tackling known hindrances to godly life. If the Church accepts that it has this role in matters of 'individual' ethics – as, for example, over the question of abortion – it must also accept that it has this same role in community ethics. If the Church speaks out for legislation to protect the doctor and the pregnant woman in the matter of abortion, it must speak up for the protection of working people and minority communities within our aggressive and plural society. The Church has consistently failed in uncovering the pressures upon people in industrial and urban communities, and this failure has encouraged the general belief that the gospel of Jesus has little relevance for the working people and oppressed communities of the twentieth century. We have not identified sufficiently with the moral dilemmas imposed by our present structures of industrial and economic life. It is a failure in preaching the Word of God in an industrial age. It is the gospel of Jesus Christ which challenges every abuse of God's creation, and particularly of the abuse of man's created dignity and worth. Everything which undermines the moral integrity and value of all that God has made is challenged by this gospel. This is why the gospel challenges deprivation, oppression, captivity and poverty (Luke 4:18). That same passage implies that Christ has come to bring a new 'jubilee' from God, a restoration of justice under the hard structures which hold people 'captives' in various ways and which prevent them enjoying in full the liberty for which they were created by God.

In trying to think through the sort of theological approach which is the most instructive, as we consider political and social questions, it is worth considering the possibility that the creation/kingdom argument has polarised the discussion far too much. If it is true that our knowledge of God and of ourselves in relation to him informs and transforms our total human commitment, then there is no basic area of belief which is not pertinent to ethical decision-making. The more we know of God, the more we know of what we are called to be and to do.

GOD HAS MET US IN HISTORY

The way in which we have come to know God instructs us as we think of what we are to be and called to do, God has made himself known to us by his act and his word in history. God has spoken to us through events, in words, and supremely in his Son Jesus Christ. He has met with us to bring us into redeemed fellowship with himself and into loving fellowship with one another. God has taken action for us. His work for us is help and salvation. God's power towards us is creative, sustaining, loving and saving.

Government over the community is the exercise of power under God. Those who are called to it are brought into an office in God's order (Romans 13:1). Their power is exercised in law making and enforcing, in defending the community, and in raising revenue to do the tasks of government. Such power is to be exercised in ways which are consistent with the known character of God as he acts for us. Power in the community is to be exercised towards people creatively, sustaining their lives, protecting the weak from the intrusions of the strong, providing for the needy and creating those structures of community life which enable people to discover their vocations in God's world.

GOD AS CREATOR

The God who has met with us, is our Creator. God has created, and does sustain, the life of the whole world through Jesus Christ. To know God as Creator helps us in two important ways as we consider our political concerns. First, to see all of human life and experience embraced in God's creative purposes brings every aspect of our living in relation to God. Those, therefore, who hold positions of power in society have responsibilities which derive from the character of God's purposes in creation and God's contemporary care for his world. It is God who has provided for the care of people set in community, despite the wickedness of the world. Government is an institution under God's providential care of mankind. Therefore, those who carry office in society must exercise that office in a way which is consistent with the character of a providential God who looks after the weak and the strong, the sick and the healthy, without discrimination. Christians will, therefore, assert that there is a fundamental principle of justice to which governments have a duty. Politics is about the just exercise of power. The power of the sword, necessary in a fallen world, must be carried consistently with the call of justice. Those who carry power in the community must provide for the whole community just arrangements of material and social living, and must enforce those just arrangements in an equitable manner.

God as creator also sets limits on power. He denies the absolute to any institutions of human life. All carry power as a stewardship from God the giver of all power (John 19 :11). Therefore political institutions are not beyond basic criticism and not beyond radical change. They must be judged according to their performance in the light of their responsibilities. The Bible is unerring in its resistance of the absolute in power. Any attempt to assume functions and positions which in any sense compromise the sense of stewardship before God is resisted throughout Scripture. This is why priestly functions are denied to kings in the Old Testament and why Saul is condemned for doing Samuel's work (1 Samuel 13 :8ff). Christians in the early Church before the Constantinian revolution resisted the imperial claim to divinity as a justification for political office. Today Christians living with dictatorship or with Marxist absolutism reject the claim of the state to silence the voice of criticism and protest.

A FALLEN WORLD

The failure of man to live in obedient trust to God, enjoying the creative purposes of God, discovering love and freedom in human society, has led to the spoliation of every part of human experience. Man is tempted to corrupt the gifts of God and to turn them to immediate and selfish ends. Power, which can be used creatively in the service of people, is diverted to its own selfish ends. The stewardship in power is forgotten, and it is turned away from its purpose to human repression, to partisan ends and to violent means in its maintenance. Those who wield power are easily tempted into delusions of absolute and unlimited power – to take control, if it were possible, even over men's consciences and inner loyalties.

The complexities of power today make it even more vital that provision is made to keep the exercise of power in check. It is all too easy for governments, even in democratic systems, to further their own partisan ends by corrupt means behind a veil of secrecy. The Watergate affair in the United States gives classic warning of the way power can so easily and subtly deceive the people.[5] There need to be enforceable constitutional checks upon the activity of government. In these days of large government, the activity of government needs to be open to inspection, available to criticism. The people, acting in the public interest, must take steps to resist tyranny with its disorderly tendencies. In a democracy, the people have a public duty to provide for orderly government and to prevent the abuse of power. The type of action taken against tyrranical power will depend upon the situation. There are constitutional means for removing the Nixons of history. No such avenues are available for those who languish under the Hitlers of political life. It is difficult to say that Bonhoeffer and his contemporaries were wrong in 1944 to seek to overthrow Hitler by violent means.[6] The aim of all resistance to tyranny is to re-establish the orderly and responsible use of power for the well-being of the whole community. It is to re-establish just law over the life of the body-politic.

A WORLD REDEEMED

God's action in history, coming to its climax in Jesus Christ, is redemptive for the world. Jesus died, not for our sins only, but also for those of the whole world. In Christ God has brought in the kingdom of the new creation. In him the world is saved and restored to fellowship with God. In Christ there is hope of a new world marked by peace (Isaiah :4), fellowship (Isaiah 11 :6ff) and joy (Revelation 21 :3–4). In Christ we are given a new vision for the world in which people experience the freedom which forgiveness brings, in which they rediscover trust in relationships and service in their living. It is a new world entered through the sufferings of the Cross. It is entered through crisis and uncompromising commitment. The rich ruler had to leave his wealth, this side of the eye of the needle, to serve the poor if he was to discover the way to eternal life beyond that act of commitment to Jesus.

Christian people will always be seeking opportunity to direct the world to the new way of Jesus. The whole of life is challenged by the call of Jesus in the Gospel. So it is never satisfied with the suggestion that individual ethics can be Christian while community ethics cannot. Although it recognizes the greater power of resistance in the social, it sees the teaching of Jesus as having social impact as well as individual impact. The attack Jesus makes on unregenerate materialism, the call he makes for sacrificial living among people, the call for generosity in human relationships, can all teach a new way for the whole of man's life, inclusive of his social and community living. The Christian Gospel has a witness in the realm of politics and structures as well as at the level of my individual behaviour. In so far as I call the whole community to give up some of its wealth to meet the needs of the poor and of the deprived groups of our world, in so far as I campaign for a form of society in which structures serve the interests of the needy and protect the weak from the machinations of the strong, then I give social witness to the distinctive values of the gospel. I bear witness to the shape of the kingdom to come in the purpose of God. I am saying that this is what heaven is like and that heaven embraces the whole reality of people's lives.

This focus on the kingdom which comes in Jesus also witnesses to the radical call of the Gospel. The call of Jesus to the disciples is the call to a radical new life. The whole quality of his life witnessed to the unique call of the Gospel. In him we see love in a new way affecting relationships and attitudes. This is the nature of the kingdom which Jesus is establishing in himself. It is not enough, therefore, for the Christian to be a good citizen, he must also be among people questioning their contemporary values and calling them to the radically distinct life of the kingdom of God. The Christian man cannot avoid seeking to achieve that in his political outlook as well. Simply to maintain law and order is not enough, he must also witness to the new order and the distinctive relationships of love and forgiveness and sacrifice, which are in being in Christ. The Christian gives contemporary flesh to this new life by his willingness to identify with the community needs and causes of the poor, the weak, the alienated and the oppressed. To fail to identify in this way is to fail in an essential witness to the gospel.

This way of thinking gives witness to the essentially Christian truth that the kingdom of God has come among us in Christ in the context of our history, our material life, our community values. It can never be a form of spirituality which is unrelated to the actual causes and hopes of people's lives and historic experience.

So the Christian is not afraid to give practical witness to the basic truths of his faith. He will seek to earth his witness in the historical life of man as a political animal. He will learn from God about the nature of power and its use in the service of people. He will respect and honour the institutions which God has provided for the well-being of the whole world and he will witness to their proper use in God's order. He will be aware of the power of sin in the political structure of living and be concerned to provide forms of community life able to resist tyranny. He will live for the kingdom of Christ, ready to suffer for it, concerned to bring into the community the values and concerns of Jesus himself. His politics, therefore, are marked by realism and hope, by the ready acceptance of power and its opportunities, in the service of God the creator and redeemer of the world.

WHERE DOES THIS LEAVE US?

Above all else that we say, we have to affirm the need for vitality in the contemporary debate. All the tools which a Christian recognizes as having to do with the Word of God must be deployed. There must be *listening*. The voice of the whole Church must be heard by the whole Church. The experience, the questions, the frustrations, the agonies of the people of God coming from their several callings must be heard and understood. There must be *preaching*. The voice of the Word must be brought into every level of our community life and experience. There must be that preaching which offers sympathetic and yet searchingly critical analysis of our contemporary values and practices in society. That dialogue between the voice heard and understood and the Word preached and received is the living dialogue in which the Spirit of God is present in power and in love.

The battle is on in the Christian world against all who seek to remove the Word of God from the living world of politics and economics. It is a battle which the Church cannot afford to avoid. It is here that one of the key areas of mission and obedience is being won or lost.

The struggle of the Gospel involves us in the contemporary debate about the future shape of our society. This is a living debate which offers no easy or permanent solutions. It presents us rather with the challenge of an ever-changing social order and with the ever-contemporary meaning of the Word of God in its midst. The call of God today in the interests of stability and of justice may leave us with no alternative but to call for the return of the politician to the place of power through the extension of democracy within both the political and the economic orders.

Such a concern for God's Word in our society, if it is a true and Christian concern, will lead us finally to re-examine the way the Church as an institution shapes its life and ministry in response to its mission. How can the Church which calls on the sacred name of Jesus Christ witness within its own life to the 'humanness' of human life discovered in Christ, and to the distinctive values and life of the kingdom of God?

This debate will be searching and painful. It will divide, and yet it will create opportunity. Out of death, in Christ, God brings new life. So it is in humble faithful obedience to Jesus Christ that we must accept this as our task today.

Questions for discussion

1. Analyse who wields effective power in your local community and why: local MP, councillors, civil servants, school boards etc.

2. How readily accountable are these people?

3. What restrictions are there upon local power which cause frustration in the community in the economic, governmental, social and other fields?

4. What do you think will be the effects both of devolution of power to the regions, and centralization of power in Brussels over the EEC?

5. What problems in the practice of the Christian life does the working man face in his job, from his work, his employer, his fellow workers or his trade union?

6. Are there ways of improving the structures of industry which would remove some of these difficulties?

7. Do you think Christianity is a 'materialistic' religion? Can Christians support policies designed to produce greater wealth in our society?

8. Is it ever right for Christians to oppose the government? How far can that opposition be taken?

9. Look up Romans 13:1–10 and Revelation 13:1–10 and think through the different pictures of power presented here.

10. Read John 18:33–19:16 and consider what we can learn about political power from Jesus's encounter with Pilate.

NOTES

1. P. Stanworth and A. Giddens (Eds), *Elites and Power in British Society*, Cambridge, 1974. An analysis of Greenwich Labour Party in 1956 revealed that 92% of its supporters were working class, and 89% of its members likewise, but only 44% of its officers were working class; 45% were middle class. Labour Government Cabinets 1935–55 had 55·9% of their members from working class background, and 41.2% from a middle class background. Cabinets of 1964–70 had 35%

from working class and 62% from middle class backgrounds. There is therefore a tendency for the leadership to fail to reflect the nature of the support of the party at its grass roots.

2. Many Christians would want to say that such an aim is entirely consistent with Christian belief. Christianity encourages enterprise and is essentially a materialistic religion. Thus the aim of increasing wealth and growth in the economy cannot be questioned on theological grounds.

3. The crude facts are that ⅓ of the world's population makes use of ⅔ of its resources, while ⅔ are able to make use of only ⅓ of the resources. ⅓ of the world's population controls ⅔ of the world's wealth. ⅓ of the world's population consumes ⅔ of the world's food.

4. Volvo in Sweden changed from a production line method in car manufacture to one designed to give workers greater satisfaction in what they were doing. Each car is now produced by one team of men, who do all the work on the vehicle all the way through the production process. They have also introduced schemes for worker participation in company decision making. The company is still highly profitable and, so far, free from industrial disputes.

5. See R. Woodward and C. Bernstein, *All the President's Men*, New York, 1975.

6. See both H. Thielicke, *Theological Ethics, vol. II, Politics*, London, 1968, and E. Bethge, *Dietrich Bonhoeffer*, London, 1970.

2

The Power of the Media[1]

RAYMOND JOHNSTON
Educationist and Academic, currently a Director of the Nationwide Festival of Light

Christians are well aware that their God is in the communication business and that words, symbols and visions are part of the very stuff of their religion. By definition, therefore, the Christian Church is bound to be interested in each and every medium through which flow the ideas that influence and shape our society. There is power at work here, both for good and evil.

So too, in any purely sociological analysis of the structure of modern society, the mass media will figure as a prominent feature. By 'mass media' we commonly mean broadcasting (television and radio); the press (national and regional, dailies and weeklies); the cinema; and the advertising industry. To these we shall add the magazine and paperback industries, and the commercial record companies.

All these channels of communication circulate, publish, distribute or broadcast material to very large numbers of people. Each message in speech, print or pictures is sent out to the millions, but originates from a source consisting of a comparatively small number of individuals. The amount of feedback from, or control by, the recipients is also comparatively small. We have, therefore, largely a one-way system out of the control of the audience, though to some extent consumers may opt with their feet, or switch off, or refuse to open their purses when the next offer comes.

The mass media, without question, represent an interlinked group of institutions to be ranked with the great power centres in the community – with government, political parties, the industrial concerns, trade unions, the law and the churches. Exposure time to the messages of the media is very high. Viewing, listening and reading are widespread and time-consuming activities. The mass media are not only the source of information to the community from the great power centres, but also largely the channel of communication between these centres themselves. It is therefore likely on this simple analysis alone that the mass media will be extremely influential in the forming of attitudes.

It is still occasionally maintained that the media have little or no effect upon those who see, read or listen. This is *prima facie* unlikely, since the whole of the educational enterprise is built on the contrary assumption, thus :—

1. most human behaviour is acquired by social learning, or 'acculturation';
2. a 'culture' is a community's pattern of transmitted knowledge and meanings, facts, values, attitudes, skills and roles;
3. the educational process is centrally one of socialization, i.e. the transmission and enrichment of the culture of a society;
4. the intention is that their attitudes and values should be changed, skills should be acquired and certain roles be learned by the young;
5. education typically uses a controlled situation in which the rising generation read, see, hear and study particular material;
6. mass media are also cultural mediators employing precisely the same techniques.

It is not surprising therefore that in both Marxist and capitalist countries the principal intrusive factor in public life is mass communication of a particular kind – the political ideology of Marxism on the one hand, the advertising of commercial products on the other. Both represent huge investments of time, talent and money, with the aim of influencing millions. If this is not a case of the exercising of power, it is difficult to know what is.

The danger of media power has recently been emphasized by the Labour Party:

> The growing concentration of power over the mass media is, therefore, of great concern . . . communications are coming under the control of fewer people. Concerns are spreading across the whole field of the media – television, papers, publishing, theatre, cinema, etc. A few people are in a position to impose their taste upon the masses, or to prevent the expression of certain views and to wield their considerable economic power as they think best. The potential quite clearly exists for a form of censorship every bit as undesirable as the more blatant variety utilized by some governments.[2]

In this chapter we are primarily concerned with the facts, figures and influences in the world of the mass media, and with the *power* factors which are overtly or covertly involved. It is right to acknowledge at the outset that the media have put millions in their debt. They have provided an incalculable amount of variety, colour, humour and sheer information which delights the heart, stretches the mind and enriches the imagination. Any assessment in terms of statistics and of power may easily neglect this cultural dimension and it is not our intention to minimize the recreational and educational achievements of the media, nor the sheer invigoration of humour and the unalloyed pleasure from sight and sound which they have brought to us. Evangelical Christian theology rightly affirms a proper place for relaxation and even escapism in the rhythm of everyday life, a need for which the mass media cater superbly.

Less frequently acknowledged is the positive function of the media to disturb the accepted patterns of received opinion, to provoke new approaches and fresh lines of thought. Media coverage can awaken the slumbering social conscience. Long ago William Randolph Hearst defined the journalist's job as 'comforting the afflicted and afflicting the comfortable'. However this 'gadfly potential' can be a two-edged weapon. One function which art, socially conscious reporting and documentary material share is certainly to provoke a sense of 'creative outrage'. But not all that outrages is creative, or thereby proved justified. The search for outrage can easily degenerate into sensational journalism of the worst variety. Self-indulgent writers and producers can deliberately present offensive material whose sole effect is to batter the bourgeois. It is the 'Horror Shock' headline which reminds us how often news selection and priorities are dominated by this interest.

BROADCASTING

There are just under eighteen and a half million households in Great Britain. About 10% of the population who do not live in households are in institutions of various types – hotels, hospitals, prisons, defence establishments and various types of 'home'. In 1975 there were 17.7 million TV licences taken out. Television viewing was by far the most frequently mentioned leisure time activity in the figures given for 1973 in *Social Trends*. In 1975 the overall average weekly viewing time for all persons aged 5 and over was 19.7 hours in the winter months and 15.7 in the summer. For children aged 5–14 these figures were 24 hours in the winter and 22.4 hours in the summer. In 1968 an Opinion Research Centre survey showed that nearly half the population devoted most of its leisure time to TV viewing. Official audited accounts of the BBC show an expenditure for the year 1973/4 of £141,000,000 and for the year 1974–5 of £168,000,000. The cost of Independent commercial broadcasting is greater but statistics are harder to come by. The BBC, which is often referred to as the 'public service organization' and the Independent Broadcasting Authority (IBA) also have the oversight of an increasing network of local radio stations. And of course the BBC has its own familiar four channels of sound radio with national coverage.

The total impact of the existence of all these channels of communication upon society is incalculable but must in the very nature of the case be considerable. The only questions to be asked are: on whom is the influence exerted, just how strong is it, and in what direction is it most effectively applied? Thereafter we cannot avoid a moral assessment of these effects.

Officially the functions of broadcasting are information, entertainment and education. But the complex processes of acceptance and rejection within the huge bureaucracies of broadcasting inevitably select certain items and reject others. The long-term effects of this process in a society so dependent upon radio and TV for the first two types of material (information and entertainment) must be considerable but they are of course difficult to isolate. As well as direct changes in the behaviour and attitudes of individuals or groups, 'television may provide models for identification, confer status on people and behaviour, spell out norms, define new situations, provide stereotypes, set frameworks of anticipation and indicate levels of acceptability, tolerance and approval'.[3]

In the field of information the very selection of items for (primarily) visual appeal by TV news, for example, is only one obvious type of selection. In 1972 half a random sample of adults put television as the most important source of news, and two-thirds rated it as the most credible source in that they would believe it against radio or the press.[4] Thus it seems important to recognize that even in its informative function – or perhaps especially in this department! – considerable power is in fact being exerted.

Entertainment is a more objective way of denoting the intentionally 'escape' aspect of broadcasting. But there are often educational implications also. The wider availability of opera, concert or ballet, drama, poetry and the great treasures of art, archaeology and architecture – all this we instinctively welcome at our fireside, though perhaps the rarity value of such visits in the days before broadcasting may have invested them with an intensity of appreciation and attention which they can no longer command. But it is the dominance of light entertainment, especially the dependence upon the constant stream of 'pop' products, which has caused many to speak of radio and TV 'addiction'.

A dependence upon the instinctive stimuli of rhythmic beat music and an openness to easy manipulation by the vendors of the paraphernalia of the prevailing fashions in the youth culture can hardly be desirable. After examining the results of the General Household Survey 1973 Milton Shulman writes:

> This comprehensive survey ought to nail on the head, but probably won't, the claim that TV would enhance and enlarge the quality of our lives. The argument of the TV establishment and their mouthpieces in the Commons and the Press, was that by introducing a wider range of activities into the mass consciousness – art, archaeology, music, literature, sport – viewers would acquire a taste and curiosity about them which would encourage people to take part in them and ultimately enjoy them. The precise opposite has happened. As far as participation is concerned, life becomes more restricted, less active, less wide-ranging, less adventurous.[5]

In both documentary and drama, the impact of screened violence has been a continual source of concern. In the USA the results of dozens of research projects, both those used by the Surgeon General's Report (1970) and later investigations, are summarized in *The Early Window* (Pergamon, 1974). A study of this latter work leaves no doubt that TV violence does contribute to the actual incidence of juvenile violence. Less clear-edged in definition, but extremely pervasive, are those attitudes suggested by the words 'materialism' and 'trivialization'.

The educative function of broadcasting is not simply confined to the more formally educational fare provided by Schools Broadcasting and the Open University (each of them setting a high standard in their own field, though occasionally susceptible to the intrusion of harmful or amoral material which explicitly denies the educator's responsibility for the objective evaluation of social norms). All broadcasting reinforces cultural features of one sort or another. The Social Morality Council warned that 'if there is no unifying vision, shared in common by those who operate the broadcasting services, there is no guarantee that the sum of random effects will not be a view of man and a kind of society which no responsible person would deliberately have chosen to foster'.[6] This mixed group of Christians and agnostics went on to state '. . . there is still a consensus of agreement about what is human and what is inhuman . . . a good television service will be one which avoids patterns of programming that involve a gross distortion of the human values people uphold and care for'.[7]

THE PRESS

In 1975 the daily circulation of national morning papers on weekdays was just under 14.3 million copies. Of these more than half are made up of the sales of the two picture tabloids, the *Daily Mirror* and the *Sun*, which together sell nearly 7.5 million copies. The trend since 1971 has been for Rupert Murdoch's *Sun* (3.5 million) to increase its sales – the only daily to do so, while the *Mirror* (3.9 million) drifts downwards like all other dailies. In the 'quality' bracket, the *Daily Telegraph* has a circulation of 1.3 million, and in 1974 *The Guardian* overtook *The Times*, a lead which was reduced and then lost in 1975 (both papers hover around 315,000). The circulation of the *Express* is 2.8 million, that of the *Daily Mail* 1.7 million. There are in addition about 20 provincial morning papers and about 80 provincial evening papers, with a circulation of about 2 million and 6.5 million respectively. The two London evening newspapers sell just over 1 million copies. On Sundays, three papers top the 4 million mark : the *News of the World* (5.5), the *Sunday Mirror* (4.3) and the *Sunday People* (4.2). The *Sunday Express* figure is 3.7, the *Sunday Times* 1.3, while both the *Sunday Telegraph* and *The Observer* are below 800,000. There are six provincial Sunday papers with a total circulation of 1.3 million.

We have lived longer with the press and are more accustomed to its existence and character. But it represents a formidable power bloc in society. Perhaps the most notable feature of the sales pattern is the dominance of the Murdoch empire (*Sun* plus *News of the World*) with its sensational, sex-slanted, entertainment-orientated approach. The five leading companies account for 86% of circulation, the Mirror Group (Reed International) accounting for 20% of the dailies and 40% of the Sundays, while Murdoch's News International Company produced more than 10% of the total daily sales and more than 24% of total Sunday sales (national and provincial). Socialist theory is particularly critical of the potential for abuse in this near-monopoly system and many Christians share this concern.

Though the press and broadcasting have many similarities – the few speak to the many, information and entertainment are mingled, the personnel are to a large degree interchangeable, the financial controls overlap with ITV, styles of selection, priorities and presentation are closely related – there are nevertheless significant differences. The broadcast word or image is fleeting, the printed word or image is more durable and can be scrutinized; the press presents a range of newspapers from which the reader can choose (though the choice may not be as wide as it could or should be) whereas the choice in national radio and TV programmes is restricted. The social situation of the receiver is significantly different, since TV is largely home-based, whereas the newspaper is portable and can be 'used' in train, bus, office, etc. A broadcast programme is received only in the order which the producer has determined; a newspaper can be read in any order. In addition, one pays daily or weekly for a newspaper, so that its actual cost is repeatedly emphasized; the annual licence fee is a once-for-all payment in the case of TV, thus the whole behavioural pattern of newspaper 'consumption' is different. These differences illuminate the fact established by research that the advent of TV has not affected press content and circulation to any great extent; the two media are used differently and (apparently) to some extent fulfil different needs, despite the similarity of goals when considered abstractly.

The supposed political neutrality of the broadcasting authorities is not paralleled by a similar stance in the press. Apart from perhaps *The Times*, a definite party-political stance is associated with each newspaper, though not to the exclusion of all other views. The allegiances are known, but weak and often significantly qualified. Though no newspaper has a majority of its readers supporting a party different from its own preference, yet on the rough Conservative/Socialist categorization, research in 1970 revealed that for every newspaper between 20% and 30% of readers were voters for the 'opposite' party. Seymour-Ure comments:

> The reason for this loose connection between the party preference of papers and of their readers ... appears to be that people use papers for entertainment and general information more than specific political purposes. In particular their initial choice of paper (which is important, since inertia to change papers is very high) is not made by reference to political criteria; it is a result, rather, of social class and terminal age of education.[8]

Since the press can act as advocate of particular interests and views, having no obligation to impartiality, it can wage campaigns for changes in the law, in public policy and in the way private companies or individuals conduct themselves. The many well-known successes in this field (e.g. *Sunday Times* and thalidomide) show the power of the press. This is in addition to the types of power it shares with broadcasting – fashioning stereotypes, supporting or destroying mythologies, defining the context of public debate, reinforcing or breaking the limits of 'acceptability' and so on. The Labour Party document *The People and the Media* suggests that the influence of the Press over institutions, including Parliament itself, is probably greater than its effect over public opinion as a whole (p. 20). And quite apart from the purely political influence, there are broader, hidden cultural assumptions which call for constant Christian questioning.

THE CINEMA

Three quarters of a century ago the long-dreamed-of moving picture burst upon the world. From being a dramatic novelty, an hour's escape from the humdrum confines of everyday city life, it developed into a medium which permeates the whole fabric of civilized life.

Very high rates of cinema attendance were registered during the 1939–45 war, as we might expect, but already in the late 1940s audiences were declining. In the 20 years from 1953 to 1973 Britain's cinemas' admissions declined from nearly 1276 million to just over 142 million. This accelerating decline can only be accounted for by the advent of television, and most researchers agree with the conclusion that TV was a major, though not the sole factor in this process.

The General Household Survey shows that cinema attendance falls off steeply with increasing age. Youngsters between 16 and 19 years of age show the highest participation rate (31% for boys, 38% for girls), and when analysed by socio-economic group, full-time 'students' (including school children, of course) registered a 35% participation figure.

Business, commercial and professional groups, show nearly double the percentage of cinema-goers, a complete reversal of the composition of audiences earlier in the century. There are also neat correspondences with income and education – the higher the income the greater the cinema-going, and the more extended the education the heavier the use of the cinema.

The need for a careful evaluation of the impact of film may seem at first sight to be less pressing in view of the decline in audience figures. Against this, however, a number of countervailing facts must be set. First, the smaller audiences now consist largely of young people, their attitudes, values and beliefs still fluid. Secondly, the social situation makes the cinema a peculiarly powerful psychological influence – one views in a darkened auditorium with only one light and sound source which is precisely controlled and one is largely unconscious of the presence of others. Thirdly, TV needs the cinema to satisfy its constant demand for fictional entertainment in the evening schedules. Fourthly, the cinema has developed a certain number of 'specialist' themes and styles precisely because these are not shown on TV, and these include the screening of extreme material – physical violence, horror, verbal obscenity and sexual explicitness. The cinema has made tremendous strides as an art form since it emerged as a source of popular entertainment for dwellers in drab cities and suburbs, and its powers over the emotional and intellectual lives of its viewers have increased correspondingly, thanks to the advances in psychology, in technology and in artistic mastery.

It was in fact the cinema which first began to push back the limits of what is called 'acceptability' by the gradual breaking down of the conditions of civilized reticence in public display. The complex and largely ineffective system of controls over filmed material from the standpoint of public morals has meant that the most sickening displays of violence, the most extreme forms of verbal behaviour (obscenity and blasphemy) and the most detailed exhibition of sexual behaviour (both normal and perverted) were gradually introduced during the 1960s. The process may be conveniently studied in *What the Censor Saw* (1973) by John Trevelyan, the former Secretary of the British Board of Film Censors (a non-statutory trade body whose 'certificates' have no legal status). His acknowledgements of the money-making potential of sex and violence, of the way in which commercial interests cashed in on each new vein of greater explicitness and of how the Board constantly sought to moderate film content (only to the extent that extremes were to be reached gradually, inch by inch, film by film and year by year rather than all at once) are frank admissions.

More profound but less easy to trace are those effects which de-sensitize, brutalize, increase tolerance of violence (whether physical or verbal) and induce a depersonalized, exploitative attitude into the sexual dimension of relationships. It is difficult to maintain that there are *no* effects from constant exposure to the specialized fare which the cinema now provides. Out of roughly the same number of films seen annually, in 1970 and 1971 the Board could give only 100 'U' and 100 'A' certificates, leaving 60% of feature films to the 'AA' (16%) and the 'X' (44%) categories.

It is worth noting also that obtaining entry to an 'X' film when one is 13 or 14 years of age is widely regarded as a status symbol amongst the young, and the ability to 'sit it out' (whatever the strain of the occult or violent material) a sign of courage or strength of character. Additionally the 'X' films of the late 1960s are now regular late-night television fare on both BBC and ITV and BBC figures show a significant number of children aged 12–14 still watching at 11.30 p.m.

Only a tiny percentage of cinema-goers of any age can be shown to imitate precisely what they see but the effects of brutalization and of raising the level of spectator tolerance of inhuman behaviour must be assumed to be more widespread. Harmful addiction in the case of weak or unprincipled individuals is well-known in the field of pornographic and violent literature, and it would be surprising if it did not occur in the case of films. Be that as it may, a significant percentage of the younger age-group is being frequently exposed to material presenting an image of man which lacks nobler loyalties, feeds on despair and hatred and suggests no solution beyond alienation, aggression and mindless self-assertion.

The film industry has the technical and artistic ability to produce undoubted masterpieces and this it has done on many memorable occasions and at a great variety of levels. Is it now too late to hope that the industry will turn its back on the exploitation of unnecessarily explicit material in the fields of violence and sex and explore again the human condition in all its facets with a proper combination of realism and reticence?

ADVERTISING AND THE ECONOMICS OF THE MASS MEDIA

Advertising is a powerful force behind the development of our existing media, an eager user of the newest media technology and a skilful exploiter of every kind of fad, centre of public attention, status symbol or popular figure.

Total media advertising of all the main kinds – press, TV and radio, cinema, posters plus cost of producing the advertisements themselves – is monitored by the advertisers and their trade bodies. In 1952 about £100 million was spent on these items; within four years the amount had doubled and by 1960 it had trebled, reaching £323 million. By 1964 the £400 million had been passed, by 1968 the £500 million was reached. More recent figures may be expressed in tabular fashion thus:

	£ million					
	1969	1970	1971	1972	1973	1974
All Advertising – current prices	544	554	591	708	874	904
All advertising – 1970 prices	563	554	544	604	708	667
MCA – current prices	252	250	271	311	362	348
MCA – 1970 prices	261	250	249	265	293	258
MCA as % of Consumer Expenditure	.88	.80	. 78	.79	.81	.68
MCA as % of Gross National Product	.65	.58	.56	.57	.58	.48

The initials MCA refer to Manufacturers' Consumer Advertising – i.e. promotional advertising aimed direct at the customer – and this is what the general public mean when they refer to 'advertising'.

Total advertising as a share of consumers' expenditure hovers between 1.6% and 2%, apparently varying upon a cyclical basis every four years according to the hiccoughs in the economy caused by budgetary fiscal measures.

We must now analyse the various types of advertising. In 1974 just over a quarter of the total (£228 million of £900 million) was spent on classified advertisements. If we add Government and nationalized industries, the financial sector, specific shopping guides plus the retail trade sector, and trade and technical advertising *within* each specialist field we reach a total of £552 million, or 61.3% of total advertising expenditures. The £348 million remaining represents 38.7% the so-called Manufacturers' Consumer Advertising. This is made up of food advertising, household and leisure items, drink and tobacco, toiletries and medical, automotive, tourism, holiday and entertainment, clothing and publishing. The percentage of MCA advertising in the total expenditure is slowly declining; it was 46% in 1959 compared with 41% in 1973 and 37.4% in 1974.

It is when we come to the differing extents to which the different mass media can call upon advertising revenue that the position becomes clearer. Since the advent of television in the mid–1950s, TV advertising expenditure has risen rapidly until it now stands at over £200 million per annum (1973 £210 million, 1974 £203 million), just under a quarter of all media advertising expenditure. Press advertising has shown a very marked increase, particularly in the regional newspapers, who now form the largest single element in the whole group of media advertising channels, the vast bulk of it non-MCA expenditure (mainly classified and recruitment advertising). The three great spenders upon advertising are therefore regional newspapers (30%), commercial TV (23%) and national newspapers (18%), to give the rough 1974 proportions.

We now turn to relative financial dependence upon advertising revenue. Independent TV draws 100% of its revenue from advertising, regional newspapers 73% of theirs, national newspapers about half (49%), consumer magazines 41%, trade and technical journals (with a net revenue of only £100 million) 64%. As one might expect, the 'quality dailies' with their assumed higher status and greater influence, rely upon advertising for almost 70% of their revenue whereas the popular dailies take only 37% from advertisers and make the other 63% from sales. Three out of every four pounds of the 'quality Sundays" revenue comes from advertising, whereas the 'popular Sundays" figure is again down to 37%. The four IPC women's weeklies take 55% of their revenue from advertising.

Advertising is then a community service of information, closely bound up with a free economy, which itself is closely connected with free political institutions. Only those aged over 45 can measure the justness of David Williams' powerful advocacy of the economic and political system to which advertising belongs when he writes:

> Material comfort for nearly all is now a lot nearer to becoming a norm than it was even ten years ago, and . . . this is one of society's highest achievements. And what does this have to do with advertising? A very great deal. Few, if any, of the consumable and durable products invented or developed since the war could have been made available at 'popular' prices unless they had been mass produced. Without mass advertising to create mass markets the evolvement (sic) of such products to the 'popular' price stage would take years, in some cases decades, longer than it does at present. Advertising is not essential to product development; it is absolutely essential to the kind of accelerated product exploitation that in the latter half of the twentieth century is ensuring a degree of comfort for common people that easily exceeds that enjoyed by even wealthy Edwardians.[9]

The neglect of the spiritual cannot be laid directly at the door of advertising. It may well be better laid at the door of the church which has failed to preach the God of the Bible, heaven and hell, repentance, faith and eternal life. It can be argued that a society only gets the advertising it deserves. Yet the power to commend certain patterns of spending behaviour to millions with regularity is an open invitation to orchestrate the covetousness, envy, lust and desire to dominate which lie in the heart of sinful man. The British Code of Advertising Practice is a laudable attempt to regulate the content of advertising to what is legal, decent, honest, responsible and fair, though it is more difficult to apply these standards effectively in actual practice, as complainants have discovered.

In essence there seem to be four logically distinguishable points at which objections might be made. (1) The *fact* of advertising in principle i.e. questioning the existence of the activity – this seems difficult to sustain as a characteristic Christian stance. (2) The *degree* of advertising in society – it might be tolerable and even beneficial *only* up to a certain level, after which it could become harmful. This appears to be a point Christians ought to be studying. (3) The goods and services advertised might need to be restricted to avoid harm or offence, so that questions about the *products* using advertising would always be relevant – alcohol, nicotine and contraceptive advertisements are already the focus of Christian concern. (4) The *methods* of advertising might need to be limited so that only certain channels or techniques would be employed while others would be considered excluded. Christians should consider under which headings the various objections and caveats which they wish to register fall, and then precisely what sort of limitations they advise, on what grounds and with what sanctions.

OTHER PRODUCTS

Paperbacks, pioneered in Germany before the war, were developed by Penguin and are now a mass product which has not only brought great literature, philosophy, scientific and historical works within the reach of millions, but also permitted the wide circulation of tawdry and worthless writing. The linking of a paperback to a sensational film (e.g. Last Tango in Paris, Jaws, The Exorcist, Emmanuelle) or a popular TV series (e.g. Inheritance, The Forsyte Saga, The Pallisers) is clearly a profitable enterprise and underlines once more the inter-connection between the various media. The advantage of a TV or film presentation of a classic novel or drama is that it opens the door to the riches of the printed word to millions who would otherwise know nothing of the masterpieces of literature.

Sound recording techniques have produced a booming *record* industry, more recently diversified by the advent of the tape recorder and now the portable cassette recorder. As with the paperback market, the opportunity is open to mass produce the masterpieces of great music as well as the most ephemeral productions of the 'pop' world. The latter area is closely integrated with the marketing of records, clothes and other cult items and has been attacked by both Christians and Marxists (see for example the *Black Rain-*

bow) for its unprincipled commercialism. Mass media interdependence is again evident. Radio and TV regularly cover recorded music, both concert-hall and disco fare. Radio 1 would cease to exist without the latter, Radio 3 would be drastically cut without the former. Pop groups feature on TV, a fact which must of necessity increase the sales of certain groups' records. Recording fees from the BBC make a crucial difference to the budget of all the permanent orchestras in the country. In terms of sheer affluence however, no conductor or orchestra can approach the commercial rewards from records earned by the leading pop groups of the past two decades. The Christian must enquire carefully what 'message' is conveyed by the words sung, the musical idiom, and the life-style which makes up the sedulously promoted 'image' of each group and which gains them such mass support from the teenage market.

The world of *magazines* lies midway between paperbacks and the Press, being more 'identity-conscious' than the former, less ephemeral than the latter. A handful of publishing interests controls a large proportion of these periodicals (the four leading women's magazines all come from IPC). Unlike the Press, many magazines have maintained sales in the past five years though a sizeable fall-off has occurred in conventional women's magazines (down 25%) and popular pictorial weeklies (down over a third). The most significant gains have been notched up by sexually explicit periodicals for both men and women. The top three for men all sell over 400,000, the top two for women over 300,000. In this area, especially, Christians believe that the danger of depersonalizing human sexuality is a serious one and that the rapid growth of widely available pornography is a socially unhealthy trend.

CONCLUSION

The *existence* of the booming technology of mass communications is itself a neutral thing. Used positively it offers the possibility of men and women enlarging their knowledge of the world, speaking to each other, helping each other, coming to know each other and the forging of more lasting bonds of human sympathy. However, Christian theology will underline the need to keep a firm grip of moral principle and a constant stress upon democratic accountability in relation to the mass media, since a number of dangers are evident.

As a stress factor upon personality. The very existence of mass media on the *scale* and with the *penetration* of the media in today's westernized societies does pose a problem which is distinct from any question about the use to which these media may be put. Is there a point, we may ask, at which the saturation of a society by electronic messages, print and film becomes fundamentally harmful to individuals and to society, however good the messages themselves may be? Is there a level of media availability beyond which any further increase (whether of entertainment, education, information or advertising) becomes inimical to human development? Must we not maintain that every person needs to receive at least an irreducible minimum of *personal* messages regularly addressed to him by those who know and value him for his own individual worth? Is there not a need to take greater precaution against media intrusions into private life, especially in the area of birth, sex, death and the grief surrounding personal tragedy? Would it not be better if we could relieve the stress upon both young and old by the renewal of face-to-face neighbourhood and community activities? Should we not support the Church of England Broadcasting Commission's questioning of 'the need for more television or indeed as much as we already have'?[10]

As a total network. We have already pointed out that all mass media depend for their existence upon mass audiences and therefore need to produce maximum consumer use for at least a significant part of their products. That is their very nature. What we wish to stress here however is the interconnected nature of *all* our contemporary mass media and their tendency to say or to emphasise the same thing, though in different ways and at different times. If one looks at the great centres of our communications network one discovers how closely related they are. At the level of finance, advertising completely funds ITV, and ITV seriously affects what the other channels will show at peak viewing hours, thanks to the 'firm principle' that the BBC 'should aim at holding approximately half the total audience to BBC programmes'.[11] Advertising also provides a huge slice of press finance without which the price of most papers would rise beyond the means of the majority of purchasers. Some entertainers also provide financial backing for films.

In terms of personnel there is a constant interchange between Fleet Street and the broadcasting centres and it is not surprising that a metropolitan consensus emerges so easily on many issues of the day. Add to this the products of the commercial cinema (so essential to TV schedules) and we have a further example of the linked nature of the mass media. They form a coherent bloc, not always speaking with precisely the same voice but very easily and very quickly presenting a united front, especially in matters of taste and in the creation of stereotypes.

As power structures. The dominance of two particular interests in the contemporary world – revolutionary Marxism and commercial profit – make the mass media peculiarly desirable and useful. The emergence of a unified continental and later global system of mass communications brings this possibility of total political power much closer to us. Of course there are many brakes upon this process. The great press and broadcasting bureaucracies possess, we may concede, their own inertia and impenetrability to those who wish to use them for political or financial advantage. Certainly Government control is an undesirable way to restrain mass media in a free society. There are at present serious dangers from union closed shop activities in press and broadcasting, and given the present leadership of union bodies this is clearly the danger from the left. Less often mentioned than 'worker control' is the possibility of control by a right-wing Government. Most countries who are not totalitarian are at present having problems with the organization of their media. It is important to make the distinction between accountability at law and control by government. Few would wish newspapers to be free to indulge in contempt of court, libel, blasphemy, obscenity, incitement to crime or sheer sedition without their being accountable to the law of the land in the same way that an individual is liable.

This present invulnerability of the media may prevent undesirable developments but in the 1960s we saw the immunity from criticism which the media appeared to enjoy in several respects where Christian concern had been voiced. The Christian is rightly particularly sensitive to the filtering out of moral idealism and spiritual vision from the discussion of so many areas of life (including even church life in many cases) by the attitude of brittle detachment and deprecating wit which has dominated so many discussion, advice and news comment sections of the media. Right across the board the dimension of faith and Christian moral commitment has been frequently absent. Drama has depended more and more upon the study of abrasive social and personal dilemmas, despite the success of certain well-known favourites where more positive values are glimpsed. Indeed many are convinced that the mass media have been among the major agencies responsible for the increasing paganization of British culture in recent years.

A bureaucracy develops a thick skin, and not only develops a great capacity to absorb or resist criticism, it also typically becomes unable to apologize, however great the need to do so may seem to those viewing its mistakes from outside. We learn from time to time that internally individuals are warned and even disciplined. But it is impossible to tell how often and how effectively such rebukes are administered. In the past 15 years the Christian churches almost alone have shown the capacity for public self-criticism and the ability to apologize.

Since the media today are only curbed to a limited degree by law, convention, public morality and general inertia, it would be wise for us to face without evasion the root facts of sales, box office returns and audience ratings, which, together with certain groups with quite precise political designs, are the main factors in the world of the media. It is difficult indeed for the Christian religion to flourish within a system determined by such criteria – should it even attempt to do so? Yet it was the Christian ethic which shaped the BBC in its early days through the principles of John Reith. There is a growing number of individual Christians as well as groups of Christians in broadcasting, Fleet Street and the entertainment world. They need the help and support of other Christians in prayer and by the regular, deliberate critical scrutiny (in the setting of discussion guided by the Christian conscience) of their priorities, theory and practice. The moulding effects of the great media bureaucracies on their employees are hard to resist, even when one is conscious of them. Ten years ago at Keele we made pious noises about 'encouraging Christians to develop their skills' in the media. The change is already noticeable but in reality we have hardly begun to treat the matter seriously. One thing is certain. The intellectual, moral and political health of this country is deeply involved with the future of the media. Christians should be the last people to neglect these vital connections. Nor must we make the mistake of regarding our task solely in terms of developing an explicitly evangelistic ministry through the media. Our aim is surely larger and it is to promote creatively a society and a culture which, under God, seeks to rediscover the wholeness of man made in the divine image. To that end we strive.

Questions for discussion

1. How far are we conscious of the influence of the media on our lives, and is it likely that we do not realize how much they influence us subconsciously?
2. What, if anything, ought to be done to stop the media falling into the hands of too small a group of people (e.g. government, commercial 'barons', unions etc)?
3. To what degree ought we to welcome the 'disturbing'

function of the media which stops us from growing complacent and forces us to consider the unpalatable?

4. What does the tremendous rise in circulation of the *Sun* say to the churches about their own failure to communicate effectively at the *Sun* readership level? What can your local church do to communicate at a popular level?

5. What are the pros and cons of associating advertising with mass communication media?

6. Why has the cinema been the leader in the extension of the bounds of 'acceptability', and how far is the film industry justified in seeking to survive by such methods?

7. What can be done to stop 'tele-addiction' (average viewing is 2½ hours per day) and what are *you* doing to avoid this chronic disease from crippling you?

8. What use do we make of the complaints machinery already available (Press Council, Advertising Standards Authority, BBC and IBA Complaints bodies, etc) and is something further needed?

9. 'Censorship' is a word that has become 'dirty' in our society yet most people still accept that certain ground rules need to be operated to avoid exploitation of the young, the weak and the gullible. Do you know how the present laws affecting the media stand and would you wish them to be strengthened, or relaxed?

10. What can be done to assist people in learning to resist media pressures to conform to stereotyped fashions and life-styles?

NOTES

1. I would like to acknowledge the help given by the group from which this chapter has emerged, the members of which have said they wish to be associated with it. They are Michael Saward, John Capon, John Poulton, Andrew Quicke, Gavin Reid, Eddy Stride and David Winter.
2. *The People and the Media*, 1974, p. 5.
3. J. Halloran, *The Effects of Television*, 1970, p. 19.
4. Report, *Broadcasting, Society and the Church*, 1973, p. 97.
5. Evening Standard, 5th April 1976.

6. Report, *The Future of Broadcasting*, 1973, p. 24.
7. *ibid*, p. 27.
8. C. Seymour-Ure, *The Political Impact of Mass Media*, 1974, p. 169.
9. D. Williams, *Advertising and the Social Conscience*, 1976.
10. Report, *Broadcasting, Society and the Church*, 1973, p. 77.
11. *ibid*, p. 11.

3

Education and the Law[1]

DAVID HARTE

Barrister of Gray's Inn and Lecturer in Law at the University of Newcastle-upon-Tyne

INTRODUCTION

'Inspectors and teachers are fighting out in public for the first time divergent views on the merits and weaknesses of the changes that have been taking place in the classrooms. Particularly the increasing freedom of choice offered by many teachers to young children. The professionals are debating, with the lawyers, the evidence on whether such "free choice" can or should be combined with proficiency in basic skills such as reading and writing; whether competition among children should be encouraged, and whether they should learn to obey adults. The managers and politicians are questioning the claims of many teachers that they should be able to decide those issues without considering what parents want'.[2]

Bedfordshire County Council issued an attendance order yesterday against Mr Kenneth Sibley and warned him he may be prosecuted if his son, Duncan aged 11, does not go to school . . . He commented: 'Comprehensive Schools are inferior and I have the right to choose grammar schools if I wish. It is the fault of the education committee for abolishing grammar school education'.[3]

Brewery drayman Harry Welch last night lost his appeal against a court ruling that he failed to send his daughter to school . . . Joan has turned up at school twice every day since the trouble first began but has been sent home everytime because she was wearing two sleeper earrings and a silver ring given to her by her grandmother.[4]

Such recent newspaper reports illustrate disagreements over the legal position of parents in the education of their children. In whatever ways contemporary English society resembles or differs from that of the past, English Christians face plentiful and confused moral issues in the field of education, where the framework is shaken by political conflict and faces corrosion through the general decline in national resources. Every group which struggles to control or to have a say in this framework is demonstrating its conviction that forms of schooling affect the future beliefs and behaviour of society. Christians who accept the biblical emphasis on the family will recognize the pre-eminent responsibility and interest of parents in education.[5] Such interest and responsibility is clearly shared by those concerned in providing education, teachers and administrators and by the citizen who foots the bills through rates and taxes.[6] As each Christian is part of the Body of Christ he shares a particular responsibility and concern in the education of children, especially those of believers, even if he has none of his own and is not directly involved in the educational process. The views of children themselves may receive less attention than they should be given. How significantly does the Church treat the views of children with a living faith in Christ, but who come from unbelieving homes?

The relationship of law and morality involves complex philosophical and theological considerations. However, in practical terms individual Christians and the Church as a whole need to evaluate the moral implications of specific law either existing or proposed. For a Christian, the basic criteria for judging behaviour must be ethical according to the teaching of Christ and his apostles. Judging whether particular behaviour is right or wrong is one thing; what should be done about it is another. In particular what should be the Christian attitude to the law which affects such behaviour? Parental interests and responsibilities in education present one of the many areas where a clear method of Christian ethical analysis is needed by which to construct both a critique of existing law and a pattern for changing law so that it will comply more adequately with the Christian ethic. This chapter is an attempt to analyse some of the moral implications of one important and controversial area of existing law so as to stimulate the development of clearer methods of analysis which may be used in various fields.

THE LEGAL BASIS FOR THE DUTIES AND RIGHTS OF ENGLISH PARENTS IN THE EDUCATION OF THEIR CHILDREN AS AN EXAMPLE OF SECULAR LAW AND ITS LIMITATIONS

In its 122 sections and 9 schedules, the Education Act, 1944, still provides the basis of the law governing education in England. For the most part it is concerned with providing for the administration and financing of state schools and for the supervision of independent schools, but it contains two sections which highlight the ethical issues of parental responsibility and interest in the education of children.

> S.36 lays a duty on parents to secure the education of their children : 'It shall be the duty of the parent of every child of compulsory school age to cause him to receive efficient, full-time education suitable to his age, ability and aptitude, either by regular attendance at school or otherwise'.

> S.76 provides for education to be in accordance with parents' wishes : 'In the exercise and performance of all powers and duties conferred and imposed on them by this Act (the Secretary of State) and local education authorities shall have regard to the general principle that, so far as is compatible with the provision of efficient instruction and training and the avoidance of unreasonable public expenditure pupils are to be educated in accordance with the wishes of their parents'.

These sections are to some extent filled out by other sections of the 1944 Education Act, by other legislation and by cases reported from court hearings which provide precedents that will be applied in the future. The resulting law illustrates difficulties in relating laws to Christian ethical and moral principles. This is no place to attempt an exploration of secular philosophies analysing the nature of law, but Christians start with the proposition that the secular state has a divinely appointed though limited function for maintaining social order. That order is expressed through laws which the secular power seeks to enforce. Despite its general God-given ethical authority, however, no secular state is able to operate laws which attain to Christian perfection. This is partly because of the fallen nature of those by whom the laws must be formulated and operated as of those to whom the laws must be applied. It is also the result of certain unavoidable qualities of secular law. It may be that a failure to appreciate these qualities has led some Christians to expect too much of secular law, and has hindered others from realizing the importance of a Christian contribution to the formulation of laws.

An analysis of the ethical and moral implications of the present English law concerned with parental duties and rights can illustrate some of the possible relationships of law with Christian morality. Acts fall into the following categories.

Morally required Legally required	Morally permitted Legally required	Morally forbidden Legally required
Morally required Legally permitted	Morally permitted Legally permitted	Morally forbidden Legally permitted
Morally required Legally forbidden	Morally permitted Legally forbidden	Morally forbidden Legally forbidden

These relationships may be resolved into three main groups: where morals and law positively clash in their requirements; where they coincide and where one imposes requirements but the other is neutral. These relationships will be discussed in more detail below,[7] but first the caveat must be made that such theoretical relationships are difficult to apply in practice because the Christian ethic is fundamentally different from law, even though ethical and moral principles may be expressed in forms resembling secular laws, and secular laws partly reflect underlying moral principles needed to keep society from disintegrating whether or not legislators and judges recognize the divine authority of such principles. One of the key questions which needs to be asked about any particular law is whether it is supposed to fulfil a function for which no secular law is fitted. The limitations of secular law are partly attributable to the difficulty of balancing simplicity and sensitivity.

An acceptable law must be clear and yet must provide for exceptional cases. The more sensitive it becomes to exceptional cases, the greater the complexity which it must assume.

THE ARBITRARY NATURE OF LAW

Legislators have sought to cope with the problem of complexity by introducing an element of what may be termed 'arbitrariness' either by stating the law in an arbitrarily precise manner or by permitting discretion to those left to administer it. Where it is intended to enforce a moral principle by secular law the secular law is arbitrary in this sense to the extent that it is capable of producing a result which does not express the underlying moral principle. In some cases the arbitrary law may produce a result which is just in that it does express the principle, in others it may not.

Rigidity of Law

Laws must to some extent be arbitrary if they are to provide consistent and clear solutions in given situations. Arbitrariness may consist in the rigid form in which a law is stated or in the granting of discretion to a person applying the law. Under the Education Act 1944, s.35, parents are required to cause their children who are of 'compulsory school age' to receive appropriate education.[8] Compulsory school age is arbitrarily defined[9] as between the ages of five and sixteen. For some children it might be preferable for schooling to begin or finish earlier or later than the present ages.

The ages between which education is to be compulsory may be arbitrary but they have been selected as the most satisfactory given a mass of factors which have to be balanced against each other, notably the resources available to pay for the necessary schools. These ages are not whimsical. Had they been chosen at random they might have turned out as between 2 and 6, or between 35 and 40. Such whimsical choice would belie the underlying principle of proper compulsory education for all. The principle has to be expressed in arbitrary form, but if the arbitrary form ceases to be acceptable, or if it never is accepted the very principle may be threatened. If the law imposed compulsory education on all children from their first birthday there might be more objection to the principle that the state should require compulsory education.

Legislative Discretion

Casting laws in an arbitrarily precise form is one means of making them straightforward enough to be acceptable. Whether or not it is acceptable, the form in which a statute is passed depends on the discretion of Parliament, and the arbitrary rigidity of a statute depends largely upon the arbitrary discretion of a majority in the House of Commons.[10]

The British Parliament long expressed a formal adherence to Christian principles. How far individual members in the past showed this adherence and how far they exercised their arbitrary powers in accordance with it may be debatable. However, where members of the elected House of Commons do not profess even a formal allegiance to Christianity their power to wield arbitrary discretion is certainly of no less danger. Christians have clear biblical authority for respecting the power of the State but there is also authority for challenging abuse of that power. A consensus of the population as a whole is capable of producing anti-Christian standards. Where the power to formulate laws depends upon a small group such as the majority Parliamentary party in the House of Commons, Christians may have a particular duty to challenge the power of that group.

Crucial questions seem to be: where should political decisions be made and how wide should be the powers to make them? Thus, should a government be able to impose a given system of education on the whole country where it has a general mandate based on a narrow majority in Parliament, perhaps with a minority of votes cast throughout the country?[11] What if the majority of the population disagree with the policy in question even though they regard the government imposing it as less unsatisfactory than the alternatives? To what extent is a government supported by a clear majority entitled to override the desires of a minority? However, these issues may more appropriately be discussed elsewhere. This paper is concerned with criteria for scrutinising the laws which those with the power to do so produce and seek to enforce.

Delegated Discretion

Although theoretically entitled to pass laws in any area of life in Britain, Parliament has only limited time. It therefore delegates power to make law.

If it is permitted only in narowly restricted conditions, delegated legislation may be valuable, as where a policy has to be postponed until more resources become available. Thus, by s.34 of the Education Act 1944, the Secretary of State was empowered to raise the school leaving age from 15 to 16 by a draft Order in Council.[12] Delegated legislation also allows for detail to be restricted which otherwise could clutter statutes and confuse them. It permits flexibility in adapting detail so as to make it more clearly meet the general intentions of Parliament. Thus under s.10 of the Education Act the Secretary of State was required:

> 'to make regulations prescribing the standards to which the premises of schools maintained by local education authorities are to conform'.

The latest of such regulations[13] imposed detailed rules as to, for example, sanitary facilities, fire regulations and ventilation. These regulations were introduced in 1972 to consolidate earlier ones and make them easier to use. An Act of Parliament would have been an unnecessarily elaborate method of making such simplification.

Despite its advantages the passing of delegated legislation is more submerged from public view and thus less subject to democratic control than the passing of an Act of Parliament.[14]

Yet more submerged from public view are governmental circulars, in which principles of policy are sent out to local authorities. Such may be used to order the reorganization of secondary education along particular lines, such as on comprehensive principles.[15] A local authority is under considerable pressure to obey such circulars. A private citizen even if he knows of their contents is in a weak position to challenge them.[16]

Judicial Discretion

Arbitrary precision in the laws themselves is one means of providing enforceable laws. An alternative arbitrariness may occur where an element of discretion is introduced into the application of a law. One example of such discretion is inherent in the application of all laws. The leap between a law and the facts of a case in which it is to be applied involves an exercise of discretion which essentially carries the risk of arbitrariness.

In *Baker v. Earl*[17] a mother was convicted by magistrates on four charges of unlawfully failing to comply with school attendance orders in respect of four children. She appealed first to Quarter Sessions for a re-hearing and then by stating a case to the Divisional Court of the Queen's Bench Division. The magistrates had found that the children had no lessons or prescribed course of study, though in the words of Lord Parker C.J., the mother 'prided herself that she had brought up her children extremely well and that they were just as capable of being good citizens and making their way in life as if they had been in school'. However the appeal to the Divisional Court failed without that court trying to assess whether the mother's pride was justified. Under s.36 of the Education Act the mother had to cause each child to receive 'efficient full-time education'. Whether what she had provided complied with the standard was a question of fact. The Divisional Court would not entertain a challenge to the answer given to that question by the courts below.

Had the answer of the lower courts been whimsical, doubtless it might have been challenged, but a value judgement had to be made, and by declining to meddle the Divisional Court recognized the necessarily arbitrary nature of such a judgement. Had the Court of Quarter Sessions reached the opposite conclusion that the mother was providing 'efficient full-time education' the Divisional Court could have equally firmly refused to interfere.[18]

Quasi Judicial Discretion

Judicial, like legislative powers, must contain an arbitrary element. When either are delegated to administrators this element tends to be exaggerated. Where administrators are given adjudicative functions control by the courts is minimized, so that the scope for publicity is reduced and precedents are not worked out openly for application in future cases. Such discretion may be necessary if complex activity in society is to be controlled, but it reveals that traditional judicial structures, like traditional legislative ones have their limitations.

The law does not seek to lay down detailed rules as to the type of education which a parent must cause his child to receive. Rather, a framework is provided within which local Education Authorities, the Minister of State, parents and others may either reach a consensus or battle to impose their wills under the loose supervision of the courts. Detailed rules as to the form of education which should be provided are inevitably too complex to put into the rigid forms of legislation.

Although a few provide private tuition, for most parents

the duty which the law imposes is in practice that of sending a child to school. However, this apparently simple duty is fragmented into a multiple duty of submitting a child to the syllabus and regime of a particular school. This syllabus and regime is determined under discretion allowed to Education Authorities and the Secretary of State. The parents' multiple legal duty is essentially the product of discretion; it is fluid and it is not tied to any clear legal standards laid down by Parliament or developed by the courts. Rather it is judged in individual cases by the local Education Authority or the Secretary of State.

In *Osborne v. Martin*[19] a school attendance officer successfully appealed against a mother who had been acquitted by magistrates of failing to cause her daughter to attend school without reasonable excuse. The child had been withdrawn regularly one morning a week to attend piano classes which were not provided at the school and could only be arranged by the mother on such mornings.

Salter J. in the Divisional Court stated : 'A parent is not obliged to avail himself of the free education provided by the state, if he prefers to provide privately for his child's education. But if he does avail himself of it, he must take it as a whole'.

A major issue which may become increasingly relevant is whether the wide discretions given to educational administrators are appropriate in an increasingly pluralistic society, or whether the times may demand a code enforceable in the court's defining elements of schooling upon which a parent can insist and others from which a parent can opt to exclude his children.

The form of the regime to which a parent is under a duty to submit his children is now largely determined by administrators. The manner in which the courts have opted out from this area is illustrated by the fate of s.76 of the Education Act 1944.[20] On its face this guarantees parents a say in the form to be taken by their children's education. In *Watt v Kesteven CC*[21] a Roman Catholic parent objected that the local authority was not complying with its duty towards him under s.76 in that it refused to provide accommodation for his child at a particular Catholic School. The Court of Appeal held that this duty could not be enforced by a court, but only through a complaint to the Secretary of State under procedures laid down in s.88 of the Act. It was held that even if a parent could show that his child had suffered as a result of a failure to comply with the duty there would be no remedy in damages available from the courts. However, most significantly the court demonstrated that s.76 contained only a limited right of parents to have their wishes considered. No particular status was given to those wishes. They had to be balanced against what the local authority regarded as necessary for providing efficient instruction and training generally in the area, and against the need to avoid unreasonable public expenditure.

The apparent safeguards of s.76 can therefore be overridden by the political judgements of elected local authority or central government representatives, whose decisions may in large measure be determined by non-elected civil servants. Even if it would be impracticable for parents to be given the power to enforce more specific rights in the courts, their political influence is extremely chancy.

If parents seek to unite as a political group their rights under the Act will receive no greater protection from the courts. In *Wood v London Borough of Ealing*[22] an embryo local authority, at the government's instigation, introduced a plan for turning local schools into comprehensives. As a matter of policy the local authority refused to discuss the matter with organizations such as the joint parents' committee for the local grammar schools which claimed to represent 10,000 parents. At meetings held with parents as individuals each parent was restricted to asking one question. Relief was sought from the Chancery Division of the High Court by parents alleging that the local authority had failed to comply with its duty to take account of their wishes. Goff J. rejected their arguments. In his view s.76 was concerned only with the rights of individual parents and could not be invoked by groups of parents: 'It would be wholly impracticable if s.76 meant the wishes of parents in general, since they would almost certainly not agree in most if not all cases, and would be moreover, a constantly fluctuating body'.

As five parents were objecting as individuals, Goff J. went on to hold that even they could not claim any rights to be heard. He held that the wishes of parents under s.76 need only be considered with regard to the curriculum and whether it included any, and if so what, religious instruction and whether co-educational or single sex and matters of that sort and not the size of the school or conditions of entry. So far as the wishes of parents were relevant Goff J. underlined the decision in *Watt v Kesteven CC* that they were merely factors for the authorities to take into account.

The attitude of the courts to decisions of local and central government has recently shown signs of developing. In the case of *Regina v Tameside Metropolitan Borough Council, ex parte Secretary of State for Education and Science* a newly elected majority on the Tameside Council had sought to implement their election pledge to halt the extension of a comprehensive scheme for secondary education. The Secretary of State invoked his powers under s.68 of the Education Act 1944 ordering the Comprehensive Scheme of the previous Council to proceed on the ground that he was 'satisfied' that the newly constituted Council's plans were 'unreasonable'. When the Council refused to obey his order the Secretary of State obtained an order of Mandamus from the Divisional Court to compel them to obey. However, the Court of Appeal struck out the order[23] and this was upheld in a further appeal by the Secretary of State to the House of Lords. This case is likely to be of major importance for education law and for administrative law in general.[24] Previously it seemed that courts would strike down administrative decisions which did not comply with statutory procedures or which were made in bad faith. Now, where a minister has power to veto a local government decision on the grounds that the local government decision is unreasonable it seems that the courts will supervise the exercise of that veto and will uphold the initial decision where, in the courts view, that decision is not unreasonable even though the minister does not appear to agree with it. As Lord Denning said in the Court of Appeal, a minister must not fall into the error of thinking that anyone with whom he disagrees is unreasonable. The Tameside case seems primarily to be concerned with the relationship of political decisions at the levels of local and central government. Its significance for the individual citizen is unclear. However, where a local authority makes a decision affecting the education of children in its area, parents and others disagreeing with it would seem in no stronger position than before unless they can convince a court that the decision is unreasonable. Instead, even if parents find that the minister is sympathetic to their views the courts will prevent the minister coming to order the parents' assistance with a s.68 order unless the courts agree that the local authority has been unreasonable.

MORAL VALUES CONTRASTED WITH SECULAR LAWS

Secular law has its limitations, but what is the nature of the principles which the Christian should follow?

The Christian believes that 'the creation' is good, and according to a coherent order. Human sin disrupts that order. Nevertheless, man's own conduct reveals that he has a sensitivity to God's intentions.[25] Because sin has blurred human awareness of good and evil, in the biblical account clear general principles had to be spelled out under the Mosaic covenant so that man could consciously follow them. The Mosaic law thus partakes of the limitations of secular law, although unlike the secular law its authority comes directly from God. The limitations were illustrated by the pharisees of the New Testament who tried to live simply by following the outward mandates of the law, and failed.[26] The gospel shows how, in Christ through all he did on the cross, and by the giving of his Spirit, our acceptance with God precedes the fulfilling of the law, but nevertheless leads to its fulfilment. Furthermore, the law's 'inner' meaning has been spelled out by Christ.

The freedom of the Christian from the bondage of the law has never meant that he can do as he pleases, or that the law can now be safely disobeyed.[27] On the contrary Jesus stressed the significance of law when he said that he had not come to abolish the law and the prophets but to fulfil them.[28] Rather than forgetting the principles of the law the Christian sees its underlying implications. The rule 'thou shall not murder' is arbitrary in that it deals only with the physical act of killing. Jesus spelled out the underlying principle 'but I say to you that every one who is angry with his brother shall be liable to judgement'.[29] Such an underlying principle is too general to be enforced universally because it would capture everyone and because a man's state of mind is very difficult to prove. Thus the principle is only enforced in the limited circumstances of homicide, or where lesser but nevertheless tangible harm can be demonstrated. Modern secular laws must be precise so that their application to given facts will be apparent as far as possible from their own words. Nevertheless a subjective element is present in many if not all secular judgements,[30] although for practical purposes laws often appear to be mechanically applied; that is where everyone looking at a particular decision agrees on the meaning and application of the law.

To take an extreme example, if a parent were to imprison his child of ten in an attic with adequate food and heating but no contact with any human being, it may seem that the parent would clearly be in breach of his duty under s.36 of the Education Act 1944, but for a court to find that the parent had been breaking his duty it would need to make a value judgement. If the child had not been kept in an attic but had simply been kept at home helping his parents in a commune, a court might again conclude that the parents had broken their duty, but some observers might disagree and the meaning of s.36 would seem less clear after all. In such circumstances, judges may have recourse to an imaginary consensus. 'Efficient full-time education' could be expressed as what a reasonable man regards as efficient full-time education. Even so, for a judge to decide that a reasonable man would not regard informal upbringing in a commune as enough for the requirements of the Education Act, the judge must make his own subjective assessment of what reasonable men think amounts to efficient full-time education.

If a Christian wishes to decide whether a law has produced an acceptable conclusion his touchstone must surely be the question, would Jesus have approved that result? The non-Christians may dismiss the answer to such a question as the subjective view of the Christian asking the question. However the Christian should have confidence that his judgement of secular law is more valid than the view of the non-Christian which is certainly no less subjective, for the Christian should be able to rely, not upon his personal, possibly idiosyncratic, interpretation of Scripture, but upon the principles worked out in the Church, prayerfully, from Scripture under the guidance of the Holy Spirit between the experience of Christians in all areas of life and the thought of theologians.

Christian moral and ethical principles may be expressed in forms which resemble secular laws. Under the Mosaic Covenant moral and ethical principles were directly enforced as secular laws. A modern secular society is far more complex and yet principles such as 'thou shalt not commit murder' are generally still enforced, though the definitions of such acts as murder are much more precisely specified. The fact that certain principles are so enforced is explicable in Christian terms. If they were not enforced society would collapse but to avoid this God in his grace delegates authority to secular power.[31] In England the Christian still has the same say as any other citizen in formulating the secular laws. He is part of the secular power and not merely its subject. Thus he must face the basic questions of how far he should seek to formulate and impose Christian principles in terms of law and how far he should oppose the imposition of alternative principles or philosophies.

Where Law and Christian values clash

Perhaps the relationships between law and Christian values where the Christian course of action will be clearest, is that pair of extremes where the two are in head-on conflict: either law forbids an action which Christian values require or law requires an action which Christian values preclude. Such head-on conflicts are unusual, at the moment at any rate.

It may be difficult to identify any examples of them in English educational law at present. However, should they arise, the appropriate Christian course of action would clearly seem to be one of disobedience to the secular law.[32] Nevertheless before such direct resistance became necessary or perhaps even justifiable it would have to be clear that there was a genuine conflict, and the appropriate means of resistance would need to be carefully scrutinized.

If the state were to forbid parents to teach their children from the Bible this would clearly constitute a direct conflict between parents' legal and Christian moral obligations. Currently religious worship and instruction are matters specifically entrenched in the English school curriculum by the Education Act, 1944, s.25.[33]

However if the present law on religious education were abolished and indeed if it were replaced by a law forbidding religious instruction in schools this would not constitute a head-on conflict between law and ethics. The parent could still fulfil his ethical obligation. He would merely be restricted in doing so.[34]

If school authorities were to require children to attend classes teaching a non-Christian sexual ethic, for example including the thesis that promiscuity has psychological benefits,[35] there would not be a clear clash between a Christian parent's legal and moral obligation provided the parent was left the option of withdrawing his child from such instruction. Although in these two examples there might be no direct clash for the Christian parent, in the second at any rate there would be a direct clash for the Christian teacher if he were required to teach ethically unacceptable material.

The question of whether there is a clash for the teacher arises most acutely if he is forbidden to teach Christian truths in school. In practice this involves denying part of the Gospel.

The issues of religious education and explicit sex education can be isolated and provision made for parents to withdraw their children from classes in these subjects. However, teaching may be pervaded by a general flavour unacceptable to Christians. History lessons may be designed to attract pupils to witchcraft and the occult. English literature may include books expressing depraved attitudes to sexuality. Such books may be set by examining boards so that even substantially Christian schools may find it difficult to avoid covering them.

Where unacceptable material is inculcated in primary schools it may be particularly difficult for parents to identify as young children may not realize that what is taught at school conflicts with their parents' standards. Where secondary school children are taught such material it may be difficult for parents to counteract it without inflaming the adolescent rebelliousness which is frequently involved in establishing an independent adult personality.

Where there is a conflict between Christian values and teaching in a particular school Christian parents may find that nothing short of withdrawing the child from the school will avoid that conflict.

Where Law and Christian Values Coincide

The legal and moral quality of acts may coincide in three possible forms. An act may be forbidden both morally and by the law; it may be enforced by both, or it may be neutral for both. S.36 of the Education Act on its face seems to enforce by law what is an ethical requirement, with which Christians would concur, that parents should ensure the proper education of their children. However, because of its imprecise nature this legal provision could be used to compel children to undergo education which morally was actually wrong. 'Efficient' and 'suitable', the words used to describe the education which parents are to cause their children to receive, are words begging definition. As has been shown they seem to have been left for decision in each case where they may arise at the discretion of the court. An expanded definition would be difficult to frame, especially since secular standards in this area shift continually. Moreover what is considered morally right may vary to some extent with culture and other changes in society.

From a Christian point of view it may be said that a parent is under a positive duty to ensure that his children receive proper instruction in the Christian faith. Does this duty extend to ensuring that the children take part in worship at school? In any event the existing law does not go so far as to enforce either duty. What it does is impose a positive duty on those running schools to provide for worship and instruction, and it makes it the norm that a child should attend at such worship and instruction, allowing parents to opt out by requesting that their children should be excused from religious worship or attendance. Further, parents are given the right[36] to withdraw a pupil from the school 'during such periods as are reasonably necessary for the purpose of enabling him to receive religious instruction' under alternative arrangements of the kind desired by the parent.[37]

How acceptable is this present law relating to religious instruction and worship? Politically it would hardly be possible to impose on all parents the duty to ensure that their children receive Christian education. If such a law were enacted it could not be readily enforced and would therefore tend to bring the principle it was designed to support into disrepute, but more fundamentally, does the existence of such a duty give rise to a moral requirement that if it is possible it should be enforced? To what extent should Christians seek to enforce such duties in society at large?

Where one standard is enforced whilst the other stands neutral

In the four remaining possible relationships which have been postulated between law and Christian moral values, one standard is enforced whilst the other stands neutral. Where the law stands neutral but Christian morals require either action or inaction there may be pressure from Christians to make the law coincide with moral requirements. This raises problems similar to those where law and morality coincide and there is secular pressure for the legal rules to be altered. However, here it may be said that society has survived without the enforcement of any ethical or moral principle. If it is suggested that it should only be enforced now, it may be questioned whether it is really essential.

On the other hand an act may be morally and ethically neutral but it may be either enforced or forbidden by the secular law. From the point of view of Christian ethics if the approved secular authorities proscribe certain conduct which by itself would be morally neutral, the state imposes upon it a morally binding restraint. Similarly if the state requires certain otherwise morally neutral conduct, the state makes such conduct a moral requirement.[38] Nevertheless, such rules have only a secondary moral force. Thus, if the state were to reverse them this would be unexceptionable to a Christian. It might appear that Christians can afford not to concern themselves with such neutral areas of the law. However, this is a dangerous illusion which merits particular attention at the present time.

It has been argued in this paper that secular law is inevitably arbitrary. Enforcing valid moral principles may be dangerous because of the resistance and conflict which enforcement produces. How many have rejected Christ because they have seen his church as a repressive law enforcement pressure group? Resentment is increased because only some offenders against a law are ever punished. Enforcing morally neutral principles may produce at least as much resistance, bringing the law into disrepute and preventing it from serving its proper function in the areas where it is needed.

The enforcement or forbidding of morally neutral behaviour may be designed to protect a morally important principle. The arbitrary fixing of the ages for compulsory school means that some children may be forced to go to school where such a requirement is in no one's interest, so that those who should have the benefit of school are ensured it. However, any restriction on the freedom of choice of the individual beyond what is morally essential seems insupportable. It induces frustration and resentment against the law. Rather than submitting to such restrictions it would seem important that Christians should seek out such restrictions and campaign to eliminate them.

THE MORAL ISSUE OF RESTRICTING THE SCOPE OF SECULAR LAW

The modern English non-Christian may agree with the Christian that certain conduct should be controlled in a particular way. Certain minimum rules are necessary to ensure social coherence and stability. The non-Christian may assert this from empirical observation. The Christian may agree with his observations, but explain it in terms of God's grace preserving order in his creation which has been tainted by sin. However, there are differences of opinion as to what is the minimum law required to ensure social cohesion. What is in fact required may vary from time to time and place to place. As the underlying philosophies in society diverge these differences are bound to grow. To cope with such divergencies the legislators may impose increasingly complex laws or grant ever wider discretions in the hope of maintaining control.

In addition to the minimum required for social cohesion, laws may be added to advance particular philosophies. From a Christian viewpoint, as man loses touch with God's spirit his sense of direction falters. A means of coping with this is to fall back on the security of law. Thus the pharisees added a 'hedge' about the restricted Mosaic code. Given a much more complex society, secular man has excelled himself by constructing an ever more confusing and complex system of law containing vast discretionary powers.

At present a parent who objects to the state school system is still able to opt for a totally different alternative if he can afford it. There is political pressure to eliminate this option on the basis that it is unjust that some should have the privilege of a freedom of choice which is denied to others. It is also argued that if those who have the power to influence the form taken by education are compelled to send their children to state schools then they will provide a lever which will compel the school authorities to raise standards generally. There are prominent Christians who have espoused this approach.[39] However in the existing state system there is much variety and a measure of parental choice. If the privileged, in or out of the state system, are deprived of their advantages, what evidence is there that they will help others rather than strive harder to help themselves? Is there a Christian principle which encourages putting those who are now so privileged in such a position? An alternative view is that the abolition of private alternatives would eliminate the examples which show us the faults in the state system and which generate new ideas and patterns from which the state system can benefit. In so far as private alternatives fail to constitute such examples they are no threat to the state system but still serve to channel additional resources into education, augmenting those provided through the state.

In any event, the administration of all schools depends on the exercise of discretion. Parents can not at present affect this discretion to any large extent, even in private schools. The best they can do is choose a school of which they approve. A clearer analysis of the issues involved in controlling discretion is vital; how such control can be influenced in practice, and how far it should be. This is a matter for general Christian concern. Those who are concerned to enforce any particular pattern of state education on all will not necessarily baulk at crushing ethical and moral principles in schools if they do not share them, or at enforcing principles contrary to those which they reject.

With a greater mixing in schools of children from different social backgrounds tensions are bound to increase and it may become increasingly important to distinguish the differences which involve moral principles as opposed to cultural contrasts. If some parents fail to provide home education on matters outside traditional school syllabuses, such as personal hygiene and the responsibilities of personal relations, these matters tend to be taken on by schools. If teachers handle them differently from those parents who do regard them as their concern, major conflicts may ensue.

Some Christians may resist certain legal accretions because they disagree with them in principle. Other Christians may agree with them in principle and support them. Christians may differ on the merits of social variety or class distinction, choosing their terminology to fit their viewpoint and arguing for or against compulsory comprehensive state education and the abolition of private education. The fact is, however, that on such issues Christians differ. In this particular debate the exact areas of difference need to be identified, but assuming that a genuine difference remains, and that those prevail who favour a more uniform society, the question must still be faced of whether a preferred system should be enforced by law. It may be that this question cannot be answered in absolute terms, because the answer depends on whether enforcement is necessary to preserve adequate social cohesion, and whether or not that is so will vary with other circumstances.

The use of the word 'adequate' begs the question of just how coherent society needs to be, but the term 'adequate social cohesion' may be defined as the least that is sufficient to ensure that society does not disintegrate under the natural forces of sin; for the Christian whether a particular law is necessary for this purpose must, in the last resort, be determined at a spiritual level, or as the world would say subjectively.

Thus it is suggested that those Christians who favour the legal imposition of a given system of education upon all should establish that such a law is necessary for minimal social cohesion. They may reply that this can not be proved conclusively but that they are convinced that it is so. If their view is not enforced, society will continue to disintegrate and by the time their viewpoint is accepted it will be even more difficult to implement and will cause more pain to those on whom it will then be enforced.

In such circumstances it may be that Christians should press for such a policy to be enforced. However, it may be questioned whether the procedures for introducing such law are adequate. Should such law be enforced only when there is an adequate consensus to support it? Are the present procedures of consultation, green papers, white papers, parliamentary debate and ministerial decision sufficiently developed to ascertain whether there is such a consensus, to take account of differing views, and to inform those who may not have fixed views so that they may then express their considered judgement at the time?

Even if our democratic procedures are adequate to establish a sufficient consensus behind a new piece of legislation, all that may be ensured is that the new law will not disrupt the requisite cohesion of society; but should such a law be enforced if it is not necessary for such cohesion? If, for example, the present school system does make for social divisiveness, could that problem be met other than by enforcing a uniform system of comprehensive state education? To what extent is a uniform system desirable within the fairly modern bounds of the nation state? To what extent should decisions to enforce a given system be made at a regional or local rather than at national level?

THE MORAL ISSUE OF MAINTAINING THE SCOPE OF SECULAR LAW

As the secular state has added to the law in certain areas, it has reduced it in some others which have given Christians particular concern. Thus controls on sexual activity have been lifted. In the context of the school this may be significant, for example where teachers express views on sex perhaps using filmed material, which is explicitly permissive or is not balanced by any teaching on the Christian ethical restriction of sexual activity. If the Christian should oppose new laws, unless they are necessary for minimal social cohesion, should he support the abolition of old ones unless they are necessary for the same purpose? It is suggested that in principle this is the correct approach. However, in practice a number of differences exist.

First where a new law is suggested, its advocates may argue that it is necessary to prevent social cohesion diminishing, but the fact must be that so far society has survived without such a law. Where it is sought to abolish a law the effects may take time to work out but they are bound to be uncertain. Therefore, the risk of abolishing a rule designed to protect society should not be taken lightly. Secondly in certain areas, such as sex, the Bible is particularly explicit as to what is right and what is wrong. Where the creation account or the Mosaic law clearly indicates that certain sexual behaviour is wrong, it is suggested that there is a presumption that such restrictions are particularly important for preserving the coherence of society. If such restrictions are not to be enforced generally under the law it may be the more important to control teaching so as to take account of them.

CONCLUSION

Secular law is a clumsy instrument for enforcing morality. It is essential to maintain social coherence but if it is to be effective, where it is essential, it needs to be restricted as tightly as possible. The more extensive the law becomes, the more resources are needed to enforce it and the smaller will be the proportion of it obtaining the support in society necessary, if law generally is to be respected and obeyed. It is argued here, therefore, that Christian responsibility to support the secular law involves pressing for its restriction.

Secular law is essential in enforcing certain social obligations and in balancing interests in society. It involves controlling the exercise of power. There is a need for Christians to clarify the actions which should be priorities for prevention and for enforcement.

The form taken by the educational system may affect the control of behaviour; it will also affect the freedom of choice of individuals in society. If Christians are to show social concern for individuals they must face the problem that one person's freedom of choice is affected by giving more choice to his neighbour.

A major issue for Christians is to what extent they should seek to override those with conflicting views. To some extent the answer depends on whether it is right to cause antagonism and waste effort trying to enforce any rule where one lacks the power to do so, but the more fundamental ethical considerations must be faced first.

The motivation for overriding a parent's preferences may not be in the interest of that parent and his children but of others. How far is this justified, particularly if the overriding interests are those of the person with the power to enforce the decision? Resources are limited. Is a Christian parent justified in opposing comprehensive education or bussing of children on the grounds that other children may benefit from such schemes, but his children will suffer? Is a Christian justified in insisting on bussing because some children will then go to better schools, although he knows that other children will then arbitrarily be sent to less good schools and will be denied opportunities which their parents would ensure they used to the full? Are Christian parents justified in insisting that Christian religious education should be the norm in state schools in the interests of their children although atheist parents wish to eliminate religious education?

The various levels possible in respect of the enforcement or protection of a given legal principle need to be appreciated if Christians are to take part effectively in the conflicts being waged over such principles. Should Christians aim at a school which is truly ethically neutral? Can it be said here 'he who is not against me is for me' or is this perhaps a rather strained application of these words of Jesus, bearing in mind their original context?[40] Rather is neutrality so unrealistic an aim that Christian values and Christian moral and ethical principle must usually be urged as the norm on the basis that 'he who is not for me is against me'?[41]

Therefore, should Christians seek to impose a particular ethic, albeit with the right for non-believers to opt out? Those Christians who would force all parents to send their children to state schools seem explicitly to welcome conflict as a means of improving environmental conditions. Such improvement is a major Christian concern, but in conflict people are hurt and the conflict which may be encountered may be of a wide nature. It needs also to be recognized that if the status of any particular ethical principle is to be safeguarded at a given level in this conflict, either consensus must be reached with some who do not adhere to it, or it must be imposed. Some principles may have to be sacrificed so that others may be safeguarded. For example, Christians may have to decide whether they regard it as more important that their children should not be contaminated by a false sexual ethic taught compulsorily than that there should be religious education at least included in the curriculum of every state school.

Finally, as the form of an education system affects cultural values, such as preference for individual or group activity and aesthetic sensitivity as well as being crucial to national levels of literacy and numeracy, and to more obvious moral training, Christians need to consider how important such cultural values and standards are or whether they should be sacrificed for some greater good. If cultural issues can be distinguished from fundamental issues of Christian principle, then Christians may be enabled to press for laws which allow for maximum cultural variety whilst safeguarding Christian moral principles.

Questions for discussion

1. To what extent does the present legal requirement of education for all children between 5 and 16 accord with Christian ethical principles? Could this requirement be altered so as to accord more effectively with such principles?
2. Can you identify any areas in English schools at pre-

sent where parents or teachers are required to submit children to teaching or practices which are contrary to Christian principles? Can you identify any areas where parents or teachers are forbidden to teach or involve children at such schools in matters which Christian principles require? By what means could such situations be improved?

3. Are there subjects or attitudes to issues taught or expressed in English schools which you believe should be excluded or controlled more stringently? What priority would you give to control as between these areas and what means of control would you employ?

4. Religious education and worship are compulsory by law in state schools. Is this requirement satisfactory with respect to the schools with which you are concerned?

a) What form should religious education take for children of Christian parents? How should schools be involved in such education?

b) To what extent should state schools provide and enforce religious education and organized worship for children of non-Christian parents?

5. In the schools with which you are concerned what influence do Christian parents and teachers have upon the content of teaching and the quality of the school regime? In what areas and by what means should such influence be extended or restricted?

a) How are Christian parents and teachers able to express their influence? What is the role of Parent-Teacher Associations and teachers' union branches in your experience?

b) To what extent and by what means do others besides parents and teachers control the content of teaching and the quality of school regimes in your experience?

6. Would the abolition of private schooling in our present society be compatible with Christian principles? Is it required by Christian principles? If it is compatible but not required what attitudes should Christians adopt to this issue?

a) To what extent should Christian parents be prepared to sacrifice the potential development of their own children in the interests of other children who may come from non-Christian homes?

b) Apart from abolition of private education by what means can Christians influence the educational system so as to improve the standard of education available to deprived children?

NOTES

1. I am grateful for their comments on drafts of this paper to The Revd David Holloway, The Revd Dr Bruce Kaye, The Revd Dr Christopher Lewis, John Mickleburgh, Alan Wright and Ashley Wilton.

2. Times 24.12.75 on the inquiry into the William Tyndale Primary School, Islington, by Mr Robin Auld QC. The inquiry lasted 64 days and Mr Auld's 250,000 word report commissioned by the Inner London Education Authority was published by ILEA in July 1976.

3. Times 11.10.75.

4. Newcastle Journal 3.2.76.

5. See Chapter 4, Oliver O'Donovan 'Marriage and the Family'.

6. In 1974–5 £3,486,000,000 was spent on schools alone in the UK out of a total public expenditure of £44,765,000,000 and in a year when the gross national product was £73,977,000,000.

7. See pp. 79ff.

8. Parent is defined by s.114 of the Act to include 'a guardian and every person who has the actual custody of the child'.

9. s.25 and SI 1972 No. 444.

10. In English constitutional theory Parliament has long been regarded as supreme, but the supremacy of Parliament is now largely that of the House of Commons alone since the powers of the House of Lords have been reduced to powers of discussion and of delaying legislation by the Parliament Acts 1911 and 1949. The theoretical supremacy of Parliament is currently in question since the statutory adoption of the Treaty of Rome by the European Communities Act 1972, and in the turmoil of demands for devolution.

11. On the 10th October 1974 Mr Harold Wilson's minority Labour Government was returned to power at a general election with an overall majority of three seats in the House of Commons but with a mere 34.3% of all the votes cast in the United Kingdom!

12. See above p. 69 and note 9.

13. Standards for School Premises Regulations 1972 SI 2051.

14. Under the Education Act 1944, s.44, Regulations made under

the Act are laid before Parliament for 40 days; and may be vetoed by either House during that period. A controversial matter could pass through unnoticed. If it is noticed a debate on a regulation is necessarily less thorough than the full Parliamentary procedure required for passing a Statute.

15. Viz Department of Education and Science Circular 4/74. Where such circulars are successfully opposed governments are at least compelled to resort to passing a Bill through Parliament. The Labour government which failed to impose its will over comprehensive reorganization of education by Circular has proceeded to implement its policy by a new Educational Bill.

16. In the dispute over the Tameside Comprehensive Scheme (see text p. 75) even the Parliamentary opposition in the House of Commons failed to use the procedures available to it to compel a debate on the directive from the Secretary of State for Education seeking to veto proposals by the local authority which were allegedly crucial policy of both that local authority and of the Parliamentary opposition. See Parliamentary Debates H of C 14th June 1976, col 32 and Ronald Butt 'Five absent Tories who struck despair in Tameside' Times 17th June, 1976.

17. (1960) Times Newspaper 6th February, p. 10.

18. See Bevan v Shears (1911) 2KB 937.

19. (1927) 19 JP 197.

20. Set out at p. 66 above.

21. (1955) 1 All E. R. 473.

22. (1966) 3 All Er 514. See also *Bradbury v London Borough of Enfield* (1967). 3 All ER 343 and *Lee v Department of Education and Science* (1967). 3 All ER 450 (note) where the Court of Appeal did intervene to protect the rights of parents but only to limited procedural safeguards.

23. The Times, Law Reports 26th July and 21st October 1976.

24. Notable reference works in this area of law are J. F. Garner 'Administrative Law' (1974) Butterworths 4th Ed and S. A. de Smith 'Judicial Review of Administrative Action' (1973) Stevens 3rd Ed.

25. Romans 1:19, 20; 2:14 and 26.

26. Romans 2:17ff; Galatians 3.

27. Paul dealt with this problem notably in Romans e.g. 6:15ff, and 13:8–10.

28. Matthew 5:17–20 and consider also 5:21–48.

29. Matthew 5:21ff.

30. See pp. 71ff.

31. Matthew 22:15ff; Romans 13; 1 Peter 2:13.

32. CV Acts 4:19–20; Daniel 3:12 and 6:13, and note the attitude of Revelations 17 and 18 to the state.

33. Although religious education is specifically provided for by s.25 in the Education Act 1944 no detail is given of the nature of

such education. Under s.29 and in Schedule 5 of the Act provision is made for committees to prepare agreed syllabuses for religious instruction and standing committees to advise local authorities on the carrying out of such syllabuses. However, the discretion of appointment to these committees and their vague statutory terms of reference means that there is scope for anti-christian doctrines such as those of marxist, atheistic, materialism to be made required in religious education. More insidiously, under the Law a totally distorted picture of Christianity may be presented by teachers with no faith of their own, or indeed with a positive antagonism. Thus, a statutory provision originally designed to safeguard the teaching of the Christian religion in schools may become a means of undermining faith.

34. Proponents of such restrictions on religious education in state schools argue that this is the position in e.g. the USA.

35. Films purporting to be made for the sex education of children have been made by, for example Dr Martin Cole. Such a film 'Growing Up' showing scenes of intimate sexual behaviour is reported to have been shown to girls in a school in Oxford on the approval of the Headmistress. Dr Cole has admitted that it has been shown to 13 year old children. Times 5th August 1976.

36. s.25 (5).

37. This right is subject to the local education authority being satisfied that the parent desires the child to receive such alternative instruction, that it cannot be reasonably conveniently obtained at another state school and that the alternative arrangements have been made. Here the local authority is given a quasi judicial function which could enable it to thwart a parent desiring to exercise the right.

38. Romans 13:1; 1 Peter 2:13.

39. Bishop David Sheppard *Built as a City* 1975, pp. 183f. Until others are compelled to do likewise Bishop Sheppard for one has not sent his daughter to a deprived school. He asks p. 184 'is it fair to ask a few children to take on the system until we all take it on together?'

40. Luke 9:50.

41. Mark 12:30.

4

Marriage and the Family[1]

OLIVER O'DONOVAN
Lecturer at Wycliffe Hall, Oxford, and convener of the Grove Ethics Group which produces a series of booklets on current ethical issues

To an earlier generation it might have seemed obvious that 'Marriage and Family' was the proper heading for everything there was to say about human sexuality and the relationships that arise from it. Sexual intercourse was 'the conjugal act', sex education was 'preparation for marriage', the vocation of singleness was 'not getting married'. This is not the way in which current fashion organizes the discussion. New philosophical issues about sexual polarity, new questions about behaviour, demand to be treated independently; other patterns of socio-sexual relationship are championed as valid alternatives to monogamy. Serious claims are made on behalf of sex in transient relationships (disapprovingly called 'promiscuity' hitherto) and sex without relationship altogether (pornography). And in a society which sees many marriages fail there is increasing uncertainty about what marriage itself really is, or ought to be.

From this rewriting of the agenda it is not only the advocates of *recherche* experiment who have something to gain. The traditional Christian understandings can achieve new strength and clarity from having to face questions put in a new way. At the same time, however, there is a danger that the discussion may become fragmented. Problems of marriage-breakdown can be debated without reference to a theory of sexuality, 'deviant' orientations discussed in isolation from their social and anthropological context. Essential connections can be forgotten, and conclusions drawn from too selective a view. And so, at the risk of seeming a little old-fashioned, we have preferred to keep 'marriage and family' as a reference-point in what follows, securing a coherent and biblical overview at the cost, if need be, of more thorough attention to some of the newer issues. Yet all the while we have tried to remember the context in which marriage stands, drawing out its connections with other forms of relationship, all of them making their own legitimate and autonomous claims on Christian understanding. We hope that the questions for discussion appended to this chapter will encourage Christian understanding to meet these claims more fully.

MARRIAGE AS MUTUAL COMMITMENT

The word 'marriage', like a camera with a zoom lens, can give us two different pictures of the same event. In 'close-up' it points entirely to the sexual and social commitment of two people to each other, when 'a man leaves his father and his mother and cleaves to his wife, and they become one flesh'. Seen like this, marriage is a private exchange between the partners, an undertaking towards each other expressed in words of promise ('I, Jack, take thee, Jill . . .') and in acts of love. A wider shot shows us this and something more: there is also a public communication between the couple and the community, their families, their friends, the Church and the state, by which the two of them declare that they will live within the society as man and wife, while the community recognizes and supports them. It is a matter of merely philosophical debate which of these two perspectives shows us the 'essential' marriage; and the answer will not make a great deal of difference if we keep it clear that when we marry we accept two different kinds of obligation at once, the obligations that one assumes as an individual towards one's partner on the one hand, the obligations that the couple assume towards society on the other, each set of obligations, of course, accompanied by corresponding privileges. Can the personal commitment be assumed without the communal one, for example by setting up a home informally without announcement of intent or public ratification? Even granting that such a couple genuinely intended *marriage*, and not just a domestic experiment, such an act would still be irresponsible. Society (the couple's parents, for example) has a legitimate right to expect them to deal openly. But then, too, it has something to offer them, and they are not even supporting each other by dispensing with society's support, which could help them fulfil their private undertakings of fidelity and love.

With most of the promises we make it is a matter of free decision, not only *whether* we promise, but *what*. With the promises the couple make to each other in marriage it is not so. If they marry at all, they do so on God's (and, incidentally, the state's) terms.[2] Notwithstanding the custom in some American churches of allowing the couple to write their own vows, there can be no individually-drafted form of marriage contract, no special stipulations about what they will and will not agree to. One of the things meant by the claim that marriage is of divine institution, is that God's creative gift has made the terms what they are.[3] And what they are, effectively, is not 'terms' at all, but unconditional self-offering. The *conditional* acceptance of a wife implied by the Deuteronomic divorce law – 'if she finds no favour in his eyes because he has found some indecency in her' – is said by Jesus to be other than God's original intention. Even more strikingly, the unconditional sacrifice of Christ himself for his Church is presented by St Paul as the pattern for married love.[4] In offering to share themselves physically, psychologically, socially, spiritually, they will go to the point of suffering if need be.

And yet, because the offer is bilateral and reciprocal, there remains an unpredictability about how it will work out. Although the terms of every marriage are prescribed, and in that way each new marriage is just like every other marriage, there is a sense in which each marriage is quite unique. It is not that one has offered to give and the other has agreed to take; *both* have offered to give, and so, if the couple are sensitive to the implications of their promise, there will be no ruthless hurrying to the limit of what is permitted. The taking will be gentle, tentative and respectful. They walk a well-beaten track, and yet every step is exploratory, discovering a way of walking it which has never been discovered before. Each partner has offered the sacrifice of himself for the partner's sake, and if that offer were not made the marriage could not begin. Yet the marriage grows only as the sacrifice is *not* insisted on, so that the marriage becomes a context in which the couple's individuality, *as* a couple and *as* individuals, can flourish.

A second thing that is meant by the claim that marriage is of divine institution, 'in the time of man's innocency', is that it is, simply and for itself, a good thing, a feature of human behaviour that requires no apology or defence, not a compromise or a second-best. As Kierkegaard observed, there is an absurdity about 'the need to decide to marry – for *reasons*'. The utilitarian perspective on marriage is likely to prove destructive of it, as the intrinsic value of marriage itself will be forgotten in the search for its beneficial results. The traditional doctrine of the 'three goods' of marriage (as stated in the preamble to the Marriage Service) was not intended to be understood in the utilitarian sense, as an account of what marriage was to *achieve*; rather it tried to state what marriage *is*, using a pattern of analysis which, though not itself biblical, draws heavily on biblical material.[5] We may think of it as the I-We-They structure of the relationship; marriage has importance as *a state of the individual*, meeting personal need, as *the union of a couple* in a reciprocal partnership of mutual trust and love, and as *the basis of a wider community*, the home into which children are born and in which they will be cared for. Each of these 'three goods', in its own way, is what marriage is, and any order in which they are stated must be arbitrary. The long tradition which has ascribed a priority in value to the good of children is now rightly viewed with suspicion.

Each of these values can be appreciated equally in the sexual and the social life of a marriage. The individual's moral need (the 'remedy for sin' is simply a reinterpretation in moral terms of the emotional need identified in Genesis) is met as much by the discipline of a structured domestic relationship as by the special relief afforded to sexual frustration. The union of the couple is fostered and strengthened equally by the sharing of physical love and by co-operation in the task of setting up a home. The blessing of a family is a fulfilment both to the acts of generation and to the growth of affection in domestic life. To divide the three goods up between the social and the sexual, as though the bed were good for one thing and the board for something quite different, must obscure the true psychodynamics of marriage. This mistake is the source of the Roman Catholic misconception which has led to the prohibition of artificial contraception : the sexual life of the couple has been associated too exclusively with the good of the family, and it has been forgotten that for humans, as for other pair-bonding animals, sexual activity also serves to secure the union, and occurs, entirely 'naturally', more frequently than its strictly reproductive function would demand. Since the Lambeth Conference of 1930 the Anglican churches have accepted the responsible use of artificial contraception as a proper means of 'planned parenthood', and this is entirely right. Protestant thinking, however, is equally liable to fragment the values of marriage, though in the opposite direction, by associating the sexual life too exclusively with the unitive good, as though its connection with procreation were purely accidental.[6]

These multifaceted values make it possible for marriages to grow and change, different aspects assuming new importance at different times, without the basic structure of the institution being lost. At the beginning it is natural enough that a couple should delight more in the 'I' and the 'We' than in the prospect of 'They'. Parenthood, which supposes a certain measure of maturity and stability in the relationship, may appear rather formidable. As they grow into their marriage, their desire to be parents will probably grow too. But this does not mean that the starting-point is left behind; constantly they return to their shared fellowship with a new understanding of each other won from their joint enterprise. As the children grow and leave home, the marriage again enters new phases with new opportunities. A man does not leave his father and his mother and cleave to his wife in the space of a day and a night.

If it is a virtue of our contraceptive age that it can free modern couples from the brutally sudden plunge into pregnancy that their predecessors knew, it may be its drawback that the timid can tremble nervously on the brink for too long. Without returning to an un-biblical exaltation of parenthood as the *primary* glory of marriage, we may need to reaffirm the understanding that it is an *integral part* of that glory. To enter marriage should presuppose an openness to this good, when and as it is safe and wise to accept it. A decision to regard parenthood as an inconvenience to be avoided would close the door, not to an experience incidental to marriage, but to one central aspect of it, and this in turn would have implications for the couple's openness to the other aspects. What is at stake is not the brute fact of physical procreation itself, but that married love should be outward-looking. And that is why those who cannot have children, or for whom it would be imprudent to try, or who take very seriously their responsibility to limit population-growth, are not excluded from fulfilment in this aspect of their marriage, even though the privilege of physical procreation may be denied them. If they are young enough to be parents, the solution of adoption (though it has its own difficulties) is one which, by capitalizing on personal disappointment to meet someone else's need as well as their own, should have a special attraction for Christ's followers. But there are other ways in which a couple may build a family around them, by taking into their home, in shorter or longer-term commitments, children, young people or older people, who need a home and whose presence can enrich it. Such possibilities are not limited to those who cannot have children of their own, of course. Parents who would value a larger family than the average could well augment their natural family in this way, making their home a sphere of ministry and a place of wider community than the 'nuclear' family can usually encompass.

MARRIAGE AND SOCIETY

To trace lines of connection between the principles which govern marriage and other patterns of human relationship is a hazardous task which must be tackled with some caution. Marriage is in some ways simply unparalleled, and to impress its structure relentlessly on all kinds of human fellowship would be to deny the particular glory of the one and the autonomy of the others. And yet the attempt is irresistible. There is a question which, in one form or another, will continually demand to be answered. In the terms of Genesis it could be framed like this : when God said, 'It is not good for man to be alone', diagnosing Adam's need as the lack of human relationship, why did he not solve the problem by providing some drinking companions to while away his leisure hours, or a small boy to help him sweep up the leaves in the garden? These would have been perfectly valid and genuinely human forms of relationship. If God's decree that Adam should have a wife instead was fundamentally well-advised, not a joke or the result of a throw of angelic dice, it suggests that this particular relationship stands in some kind of archetypal position *vis à vis* the others. If we don't like that way of putting the question, we can ask instead why the term 'relationship' is often used as a euphemism for sexually significant friendship. Or we can face the question in the personally anxious form in which so many face it : can I have *the same fulfilment* without marrying that I could have if I were married? In what follows we identify three characteristics of the marriage relationship which may have wider implications.

PHYSICAL AND SOCIAL

First, *the harmonizing of the social and the sexual.* If marriage is a relationship in which the physical expressions of emotion and the social patterns of a shared life are synthesized into a unified pattern, this is surely because a right coordination between body and mind is the dominant philosophical motif governing Christian sexual ethics as a whole. St Paul's argument in 1 Corinthians 6, a passage of central importance, can be summed up: 'You can't give your body to a prostitute and your soul to God, because the prostitute takes the soul with the body and God demands the body with the soul'. Christian disapproval of sexual intercourse outside marriage, something which must appear quite arbitrary to the secular dualist (for what does it matter where I seek my physical satisfaction if I remain faithful at the 'deepest' level?) makes sense in the context of a theologically-based evaluation of the human body. The Incarnation, Resurrection and Ascension of Christ, the tokens of God's serious dealing with the human body, mean not only that the body is good (excluding false shame), but that it is *meaningful* in personal communication. Sexual intercourse intrinsically conveys the full and unreserved commitment of self to other which finds its social embodiment in marriage. Its meaning is not confined to the expression of present emotion ('I love you'), but of emotion crystallized into promise ('I *will* love you'). Its use apart from *that* meaning is, intentionally or not, a use to deceive.[7]

This has obvious implications for an ethic of courtship, in which the demand for self-control arises out of the remaining uncertainty in the mind of each as to whether he can honestly make this commitment to the other. The question about lesser acts of physical affection is a more complicated one, because although these too have meaning, the meaning is more likely to vary from culture to culture, sub-culture to sub-culture and indeed from couple to couple. The morality of these acts lies in what they express, but there is plenty of room for disagreement about what they do express. Genuine concern not to cause hurtful emotional misunderstanding will usually suggest restraint. A respect for social convention has a special place here, not simply because one ought not to be needlessly shocking, but because in the early stages of a friendship it is the only point of reference by which each can understand the other's meaning. What means what in the range of small gestures of affection will be determined very largely by what is socially agreed. However, when all that is necessary has been said in favour of caution in courtship, and without encouraging a socially distasteful flamboyance, too much inhibition can be as bad as too little. The single life and its relationships are unnecessarily impoverished if the natural gestures of affection are always avoided for fear of misconstruction. Expressions of friendship between men which caused even our Victorian ancestors no embarrassment have fallen victim to the assumption that anything and everything is a homosexual advance. We need to remember that the handclasp, the embrace, even the 'holy kiss' all have their place in social contacts quite independent of courtship and marriage.

SEXUAL COMPLEMENTARITY

Secondly, *the complementarity of male and female* in marriage poses some difficult questions about the social encounters of the two sexes in general. The closer to mating, the more polarized the sex-roles. In lovemaking itself man and woman have their different activities, and they know it. In courtship it is a notorious source of jokes that the pair will unconsciously tend to conform to the 'model' man and woman. In married life itself, though it is true that marriage must be 'without pretending', there has to be some acceptance of role, discovering oneself as husband or wife, father or mother. As with all good roles, no two interpretations will be exactly alike, and there is plenty of scope for individuality. Nevertheless, learning the role is part of caring : a response to what the partner needs in a husband or a wife, and to what the children need in a mother or father.[8]

The difficulties arise when we ask how much this polar complementarity should be reflected in the structure of social life, both domestic and public. The New Testament (again, and notoriously, in the person of St Paul) assumes that there will be places other than the bedroom in which men and women assume consciously differentiated roles. They will do so in the affairs of the home, in which the wife is to 'submit' to her husband (Eph. 5 :22ff) as head. They will do so even outside the context of family life, since man is 'head' of woman in some sense in quite another context, when the Church is at worship (1 Corinthians 11 :2ff).[9] It is a matter much in need of discussion how, if at all, this concept of a more extended role-differentiation can be implemented in modern social conditions. For example, is it acceptable for a husband to stay at home with the children while the wife is out at work? Or that a family home should be situated to suit the wife's rather than the husband's career? Or does the concept even cast doubt on the propriety of dual-career families altogether?

And what of relationships in wider society, at work for example? There has been a marked swing in popular philosophy. Some time ago, under the influence of Freud, we were encouraged to recognize the element of sexuality in all our relationships, so that the female boss became a mother-figure, while today, under the influence of a revived feminism, we are encouraged to discount it altogether – she is just another 'person'. Probably we should neither discount it entirely nor allow it the last word. There may, in fact, be genuine differences of perception between the sexes, the woman finding it easier to forget that her subordinate is a man than he does to forget that she is a woman. If this (generalization!) is at all true, then sensitivity demands that each should be aware of the other's view of the relationship and make allowances. There is no reason why the differentiation should not find expression in a working context in terms of the social courtesies and graces, even when it ought not to be allowed to affect the shape of the structures.

It would be a mistake so to focus attention on man-woman relationships as to forget the corresponding patterns of relationship between members of the same sex. In a wide sense of the word, these are 'sexual' relationships too; it is the awareness of sexual sameness that gives them their distinctive value, the sense of being colleagues, of looking at life from the same angle. A mature human being needs relationships of both kinds – and, we may add, across a wide age-range – whether he is married or single. We may laugh at 'hen parties' and 'boring men's talk', but we value them just the same. It is a false philosophy which regards 'heterosexual' and 'homosexual' relationships as alternatives, exclusive of each other. A proper discussion of homosexuality, with all its pastoral and psychological complexities, lies outside the scope of this survey, but we must include the observation that, though genital love-making between members of the same sex represents a distortion of God's purposes for human sexuality, warm and emotional friendship does not, and is entirely compatible with the so-called 'heterosexual' orientation. The tragedy of the homosexual lies not in what he has, but in what he has lost.

THE SINGLE LIFE

Thirdly, we turn back to the *I-We-They* structure of the relationship. In marriage, we have said, an individual need is met, a union of two is secured, and the basis is laid for a wider sharing in community. Do all these values have to be denied in the single life? One of them obviously does : the single life is what it is because there is no dominating and exclusive relationship around which others are grouped. But what is lost in terms of 'We' may be recovered in terms both of 'I' and of 'They'. The security of the individual and his capacity for outward-going relationships can be fully expressed in the lives of those who have not married and of those who, by widowhood or desertion, are married no longer.

True, the personal security and fulfilment experienced by the single person is won *at the cost* of one tendency of his human nature. It supposes frustration, by individual endowment, circumstance or resolve, of a desire that is common to the race.[10] Nevertheless, a person is more than the sum of his human desires; he is a unique individuality with a unique calling. And for some it may be that the individual potential can only be realized at this cost, the denial of marriage being the door into a fuller exploration and discovery of the self in its relation to God. Freedom from marriage becomes freedom for the inner life. Together with these possibilities for the enhancement of the 'I' there are others; the freedom may be turned outwards, to the 'They' world of work and people, yielding a greater availability for a wider range of relationships, more involvement with the needs of society and the Church, more freedom to move in response to a call for help or a summons from the Spirit of God. The relationships of such a life, less focussed and intense but more wide-ranging, can be emotionally demanding and fulfilling as much as the others. Attitudes to the single life have varied very sharply in Christian history, the middle ages (and to a lesser extent the nineteenth century) tending to romanticize it, our own age inclining to pity it. St Paul, whose enthusiasm for the single life has made him no friends in an age of marrying and giving in marriage, referred the matter back to the particular vocation of individuals: 'Everyone has his own gift, one this way, the other that.'[11]

Within the life of the Church the paths of the single and the married should not be allowed to diverge. The shared life of the Christian community must become a context in which the differing gifts can be used *for each other*. There is much still to be learned about this. Are the homes of married Christians an added support for the single? Is the availability of the single Christian put at the disposal of his married friends, for 'babysitting' duties and the like? And what is true of the mutual support of married and single needs to be true in a wider way of the care exercised by the married and the single for each other, so that nobody's home life becomes completely cut off from support and help. There is an important place here for Christians with a gift for marriage guidance counselling, a gift which needs to be exercised within, as well as outside, the limits of the Church fellowship. And yet this must not suggest that pastoral care for the problems of the home is to be merely a fire-engine, ready to rush to the scene of a serious conflagration. Nor is it enough even to add 'boy and girlfriend' talks to the Young People and 'wedding interviews' with engaged couples. Important as all these are, they must be supplemented with a constant experience of the Church's fellowship as a sustaining, healing and nurturing force, so that strains do not beget crises and minor crises do not escalate into major ones.

MARRIAGE BREAKDOWN

In the Synoptic Gospels the discussion of marriage is largely concerned with the problem of its dissolution; and so our attention is directed to two features of marriage which are quite special to it, its permanence and its exclusiveness.

The Church of England appears to be committed to the view, commonly accepted in the Catholic tradition of Christian thought, that marriage is 'indissoluble', i.e. that it *cannot* be broken and that once a couple are married they are married 'till death us do part'.[12] There are, in our opinion, no scriptural grounds for believing this. What the New Testament does teach, with qualifications to be noted later, is that marriage *ought not* to be broken, that divorce is (not an impossibility but) a sin.[31]

The strictly logical consequence of the indissolubilist view would be that no divorce proceedings should be allowed by the state, and that, if they are, no Christian person should take advantage of them. It is, however, completely compatible with this view that the state should provide for decrees of *nullity*, where there are good grounds for saying that a marriage never came into existence.[14] And so there has been a tendency among Catholic Anglican thinkers of a liberal turn of mind to extend the notion of nullity speculatively, allowing it to be said, on the basis of subsequent developments within the marriage, not that there never was a marriage, but simply that there is *now* no marriage recognized by the Church. Thus this tradition has come to accept the idea of irretrievable breakdown as an adequate basis for legal dissolution of a bond which, from a religious and moral point of view, is deemed non-existent. This train of thought, together with its conclusions, was well illustrated by the controversial document, *Marriage, Divorce and the Church* (1971).

Our own views may at first blush seem rather similar, and indeed the practical conclusions could be the same; but the differences, though theoretical, are of some importance for the general moral outlook. The liberal Catholic, inheriting from a much more masculine conservative Catholicism the superstition that marriages cannot be pulled apart by the activity of man, inclines to suggest that marriage breakdown 'just happens'. The New Testament, on the other hand, views divorce as a deed for which man is answerable to the judgement of God. It gives no support for that sad fatalism which hopes, with prayers and crossed fingers, that things will somehow 'work out'. If a marriage ends up in pieces, it is not due to some mysterious failure on God's part to glue the couple together securely, but because one of the partners, probably both, perhaps also someone outside the partnership, has acted irresponsibly towards it. To insist on this point is not to argue for any *disciplinary* enquiry into marriage breakdowns within the Church (this could make a difficult pastoral task more difficult still), but simply to encourage the partners themselves to face the truth about themselves honestly, and not to hide behind fatalist evasions.

Having made this point, however, we can agree that in a less than obedient society some laws to regulate and enable divorce are a necessity. We can agree, too, that from a legal point of view (without saying anything about the correct moral evaluation) the category of irretrievable breakdown has considerable advantages.[15] We can even go on to say that there are circumstances in which a Christian might properly consider taking advantage of the divorce law. It is worth pausing to consider what these circumstances might be.

The New Testament seems to envisage two exceptions to the general rule that divorce is sinful: one, noted in St Matthew's Gospel, is the case of adultery, the other, noted by St Paul, is that of desertion.[16] In either case it is assumed to be the innocent party to the matrimonial offence who has the moral right to the option of divorce. There is no suggestion in either case that he has any obligation to take the option up. We may properly treat these cases as paradigms and extend the principle to other major forms of matrimonial offence, extreme cruelty for example. But quite a different moral issue is raised in cases where there is no such self-evident offence. Could a Christian couple consistently decide to separate simply on the grounds that they were hurting each other so badly that they could have no future together? The best way of making a case for this would be to say that the 'divorce', in a moral sense, had *already* taken place in that the sin of rejection and repudiation had already been committed, committed moreover in such a way that matters were now beyond repair. This would not merely be a claim that the marriage had 'broken down'; it would admit that it had culpably *been* broken, and that neither penitence nor good will could now retrieve it. Whether such a proposal lies within the spirit of the New Testament principles we must leave open for further debate.

And what if a person *has* been divorced, rightly or wrongly? Is there any good moral reason for him to deny himself the possibility of remarriage? Five arguments against remarriage might suggest themselves to him: (1) the indissolubilist argument, that, divorced or no, he is, morally and in the sight of God, still married to his old partner; (2) an argument based on the marriage vows, that having sworn to be faithful to *that* partner for life, he is in no position to make a similar promise to another one; (3) an argument based on the possibility that he may still be able to restore his old marriage; (4) an argument that having proved faithless to his partner in divorce, it would add insult to injury to remarry; (5) an argument based on the poor prognosis for the second marriage. The first argument stands or falls with the indissolubilist position, which we believe to be mistaken. The second is really an elaboration of it. The vow was *one* vow, a promise to *marry*; the destruction of the marriage was *one* destruction (thus the Synoptic Gospels take divorce and remarriage together as a single offence), and once the marriage was broken decisively the vow was broken with it. There can be no distinct obligation to respect the vows apart from respecting the marriage. The third argument will hold good in some cases, and when it does it should be absolutely decisive; but there will also be cases in which there is no hope of restoration. The fourth argument is persuasive in a particular kind of divorce, the one which seems to have been in Jesus's mind, that which was provoked by the appearance of a 'third party'. In such a case remarriage simply regularizes adultery; but not every divorce is of this kind. The fifth argument will be more convincing in some cases than in others; together with a healthy and realistic scepticism, we must also consider the possibility of genuine new birth and moral transformation.

In conclusion, then, we cannot dogmatically assert that the desire to remarry is one which a divorced Christian should never entertain. It will not always be an *additional* wrong to remarry, and there are times (for a father with a young family, for example) when there could be strong arguments in favour. But here there is room for caution. To say that remarriage may be justified in some cases is not to say that it is always justified; and to say that it may be right for some divorced persons to remarry is not to say that the Church would be right to accept responsibility for solemnizing the marriage. The Church has more to think about than the justice of the particular case. It has to consider whether it can find a practicable way of drawing the line at the justified case and not being forced to solemnize what its Lord called adultery. It has to consider whether a decision to solemnize even justified remarriages will be generally misconstrued by the public, Christian and pagan, and so compromise its witness to God's standard in marriage. And it has to consider whether solemnizing remarriage is the *only* adequate expression it can offer of the compassion and forgiveness which it must show in Christ's name to penitent sinners. We cannot commit ourselves either to supporting or opposing a change in the present practice of refusing to remarry; for too much depends on the details of any scheme that may be put forward. But we would like to suggest, for discussion's sake, that if the Church is presented with a straight choice between the present practice and an indiscriminate acceptance of remarriages, it might be a lesser evil to remarry none than to remarry all. Easier (after all) for the disciple of Jesus to explain to a couple why he must send them to the register office, than to explain to his Lord how he came to don scarf or stole to preside at the nuptials of Herod and Herodias.

Questions for discussion

1. How Christian is planned parenthood? Can it ever be right for a Christian to enter marriage with a firm decision never to have children?
2. How would you answer the argument that 'It's foolish to marry until you have proved yourselves sexually compatible'?
3. 'Can I have the same satisfaction without marrying that I could have if I were married'? How would you answer that question?
4. Are heterosexual and homosexual relationships acceptable alternatives?
5. Should men and women have distinctive roles in their relationship (a) in society, and (b) in marriage?
6. What part should be played by (a) the home; (b) the school and (c) the Church in sex education and preparation for marriage?
7. What does a child need (a) in a father and (b) in a mother?
8. The Russians have communes and Israelis Kibbutzim. Is the family unit really necessary?
9. Is the Church too often just a 'fire-engine' when marriages break down? In what practical ways can your church's fellowship be 'a sustaining, healing and nurturing force' to prevent divorce, support marriage and strengthen family life?
10. Can a Christian regard a divorce decree as a licence to remarry?

NOTES

1. The contents of this paper represent the findings of a working-party on which the following served with the author: Mrs J. Cundy (lawyer and housewife, London), Mrs Jill Dann (housewife, member of the General Synod's Commission on Marriage), The Revd David Field (lecturer Oak Hill Theological College), Mr O. R. Johnston (Director, Festival of Light), Dr R. A. E. Spilling (general practitioner, Oxford), The Revd John Wesson (then Chaplain, Polytechnic of Central London), Mrs Jeanne Wesson (counsellor and housewife, London). The working party received valued assistance from Miss Joyce Baldwin (Associate Principal, Trinity College, Bristol).

2. The form of the ceremony, of course, is entirely variable; only the content of the covenant is invariable. Thus the Christian tradition, both Catholic and Protestant, has recognized marriages contracted by secular, or even pagan rites as valid, provided only that they imply the commitment to lifelong monogamous union.

3. Not, as wrongly interpreted by successive Prayer Books, that each and every marriage is a separate and individual work of God. 'Those whom God has joined . . .' is, of course, a romantic distortion of the synoptists' 'That which God has joined . . . ', i.e. the *institution* of marriage (Mark 10:9). The doctrine of providence certainly allows us to see God at work in the particular case as well as in the universal, but that is not what the text is saying.

4. Deuteronomy 24:1; Mark 10:5f; cf Matthew 19:8; Ephesians 5:25ff.

5. The doctrine seems to have originated with Augustine (*De bono coniugali* 24.32, and many other references) and to have been universally accepted in the Western church. For the 'first good' of children, cf. Genesis 1:28, Psalm 127:3ff; for the 'second good', the remedy for sin, see especially 1 Corinthians 7:1–9, 36–38; for the 'third good', the bond of mutual fidelity, see Genesis 2:18ff, Ephesians 5:22ff. Augustine cannot be acquitted of maintaining the priority of the first good, though it may mitigate the offence that this was the feature of the doctrine which he received from his predecessors, e.g. Justin and Clement of Alexandria. Still maintained by the Lambeth Conference in 1930 (resolution 13), the priority of the first good was decisively repudiated by the Second Vatican Council (*Gaudium et Spes* 50).

6. Paul VI's *Humanae Vitae* (1968) is still the authoritative Roman statement on the matter, stating that 'each and every marriage act must remain open to the transmission of life' (section 11). Yet 'it is licit to take into account the natural rhythms immanent in the generative functions . . . and in this way to regulate birth.' Pro-

testants continue to be puzzled about how such deliberately infertile marriage acts are still said to be 'open to the transmission of life'. The fact that contraception is *as such* morally unproblematic should not hide the fact that its widespread use can foster unhealthy attitudes. And that not only by making fornication easier. It is all too easy for conscientious 'planned parents' to forget that their children are still 'a gift of the Lord', not summoned into being by parental *fiat*. And certain types of contraceptive method raise special moral problems. Christians could well decide to avoid on principle any that are shown to operate as post-conceptive abortifacients. The use of sterilization as a method of contraception (i.e. where it is not medically indicated), though free from moral objections in itself, nevertheless raises issues of moral concern. Still for all practical purposes irreversible, it closes future options decisively; what about widowhood, death of existing children, and so on?

7. This is illustrated by the curious but significant tradition in law that unconsummated marriages can be annulled, as though the words of promise had only a *provisional* force until confirmed by a promise in act. This does not mean, of course, that those incapable of full sexual intercourse *cannot* marry, for in such a circumstance other forms of physical endearment could carry the same meaning.

8. The popular philosophy that there is no such thing as pure male or pure female but only intermediate points on a spectrum is based on a confusion of four quite different facts. It is true (a) that in all fully developed males and females there are vestiges of the undeveloped gonads of the opposite sex, and that in rare cases a child may be born with indeterminate or misleading gonads; (b) that there are (very rare) instances of genetic indeterminacy of sex. It is also true, but an entirely different matter, that, (c) a large amount of sexual behaviour is learned in early childhood, so that it is possible for someone to acquire a 'gender-role' at variance with his physical sexuality. All this does not amount to saying that there is no such thing as the 'normal' man or woman in a medical or psychological sense. It merely establishes that conditions do occur which are, either by medical or psychological criteria, pathological. That established, we may add, (d) that *within* the parameters of normal sexual development there is a happy variety of taste and temperament to be encountered, so that generalizations on this level are to be treated as generalizations merely, not as cast-iron rules. But we must learn to distinguish natural variations in behaviour from pathological conditions.

9. In order that St Paul should not be misjudged, we must note:—(a) that this relational ordering of male and female presupposes a fundamental generic equality (1 Corinthians 11:11f); and (b) that the 'submission' of the wife is a special case of a 'submission' of all Christians to one another, and complements a husband's love that

is to be expressed in self-sacrifice (Ephesians 5:21ff, 25ff). The apostle is not an apologist for male tyranny.

10. Thus Jesus speaks of those who 'make themselves eunuchs', Matthew 19:12, vividly suggesting the measure of denial involved in the single life.

11. 1 Corinthians 7:7. This emphasis is very different from that of the 1662 Prayer Book, for example, which assigns marriage to 'such persons as have *not* the gift of continency . . .!'

12. The present position of the Church of England is expressed in an ambiguously worded Resolution of Convocation of 1938: 'This house affirms that according to God's will, declared by Our Lord, marriage is in its true principle a personal union for better or for worse, of one man with one woman, exclusive of all others on either side, and indissoluble save by death'.

13. We are unable to work the biblical arguments out in detail here, but refer readers to the relevant texts: Mark 10:1–12, Matthew 19:3–9; also Matthew 5:31ff, Luke 16:18. Paul's treatment of the issue is at 1 Corinthians 7:10ff. These texts are undoubtedly difficult to interpret in detail, though the general force is very clear. The questions to be borne in mind are:— (a) In what sense is Jesus's description of divorce-and-remarriage as 'adultery' intended? (Indissolubilist answer: absolutely literally.) (b) Why does Jesus not permit the remarriage of a divorced woman? (Indissolubilist answer: because she is still her ex-husband's wife.) (c) Does Paul intend to permit the remarriage of a deserted partner at 1 Corinthians 7:15? (Indissolubilist answer: No.) Our case rests on there being better answers to each of these questions.

14. The state currently recognizes six grounds for declaring a marriage void *ab initio* and six rendering it optionally voidable. As specified by the Matrimonial Causes Act 1973, they are: (a) consanguinity within prohibited degrees, want of age, defective formalities, a prior subsisting marriage, the parties not respectively male and female, polygamy; (b) incapacity to consummate, wilful refusal to consummate, lack of consent, insanity, one party suffering from venereal disease at time of marriage, woman pregnant at time of marriage by another man.

15. The Matrimonial Causes Act 1973 (following the Divorce Reform Act 1969) specifies five 'facts', any one of which must be proved as evidence of irretrievable breakdown: (i) that the Respondent has committed adultery and the Petitioner finds it intolerable to live with the R.; (ii) that the R. has behaved in such a way that the P. cannot reasonably be expected to live with the R.; (iii) that the R. has deserted the P. for a continuous period of two years immediately preceding presentation of the petition; (iv) that the parties have lived apart for a continuous period of at least two years, and the R. consents to a decree being granted; (v) that the parties have

lived apart for a continuous period of at least five years. The advantage of this law is that by providing other grounds than the old matrimonial 'offence' it has cut out the often disreputable and unsavoury business of proving the offence. Its disadvantage may be seen in the astronomical rise in divorce figures. In divorce, as in other things, availability seems to create demand.

16. Matthew 19:9, cf 5:32; 1 Corinthians 7:15. We do not accept the assumption that Matthew has improvised the exception in the case of adultery: it corresponds to the possibility, noted by St Mark, that a woman might divorce her husband. Cf. n. 13 above on the interpretation of 1 Corinthians 7:15.

5

The Gospel and Culture

DAVID BRONNERT
Vicar of St John's Southall and
formerly Chairman of the Evangelical Race Relations Group

THE NON-EXISTENT PAST

Many people suppose that Britain was once a culturally uniform nation, and that its development as a multi-racial, pluralistic society is post-war. There is no question that these matters have been brought to the fore by the presence of a minority from the 'New Commonwealth' in the urban centres of Britain. The presence of 'coloured' people has high-lighted many issues that existed before, drawing attention to various social conditions, and intensifying the issues of cultural and religious tolerance. The challenges are now seen to be of great importance, because of the implications of having 'visible' minorities with all the possibilities of discrimination and hostility, or variety and cultural enrichment.

However, it is essential to recognize that the matters of principle have been in existence for a very long time. There is no room for romanticizing about an 'ideal' society that existed before the period of post-war immigration, with the thought that one day it might be possible to return to that society; or, for those more realistic, an instinctive feeling that the visible newcomers are the people to be blamed for the difficulties that now confront British society. In the British Isles, there have been for a long time four different nations: the English, the Scots, the Welsh and the Irish. Associated with these nations have been differences in culture, language and religion – different varieties of Christianity have moulded each nation. The last thorough-going attempt to make a uniform society in Britain was the Act of Uniformity in 1662. Even that allowed for differences in the component nations of the United Kingdom and did not exclude the recently re-admitted Jewish minority. Nor was there the thorough-going attempt to extirpate the minorities in England such as occurred under Queen Mary. Over the subsequent years there was a growth of tolerance for the non-conformists, then much later for the Roman Catholics, and then for atheists. Although the cultural background of Britain as a whole has been Christian, allowance has been made for the Jewish minority in religious observance, in education and dietary matters.

There have also been 'coloured' minorities in Britain for a long time; an attempt to exclude them was made in 1596, there were large numbers in the eighteenth century, and in the first half of the twentieth century the major British ports had 'coloured' areas. Racial prejudice and discrimination have long roots too. The idea that once Britain was a tolerant country that always welcomed new-comers, especially refugees, is also part of the non-existent past. Huguenots, Jews, Irish and Italians have all experienced rebuff and hostility to a greater or lesser extent. So there have been differences of culture (culture covers the thought-patterns, literature, language and organization of social life of particular groups) and race (race can be defined as populations distinguished from other populations by several physical characteristics which are hereditary and are usually found in association with each other) of long standing in Britain.

The fact that no new issue of principle exists in the second half of the twentieth century does not mean that issues are therefore less important. The 'visibility' factor, that persists with those born in Britain, makes clear the vital nature of the issues.

SOCIAL JUSTICE

Scripture does not present a detailed Christian social order, but it does give clear guidance in the form of basic truths about God and man; what God requires of man in the realm of justice and humanity and brotherhood, and what God detests. The approach can be expressed in St Paul's words: 'Let each of you look not only to his own interests, but also to the interests of others'. This implies the recognition that others have value and worth equal to one's own. Other families, other communities, have value and worth equal to one's own family and community. They too are 'made in the image of God' and share in all the glory and all the shame of being human. If a Christian is to work out his responsibility towards others, he has to consider what the rights of others are, and a community has to evaluate rights and obligations for the same reason.

What rights do men possess? All men are made in the image of God and by right belong to the one human family. They have a right to the society of others in the complex web of personal, family, work and social relationships that make up a truly human existence. Men may forfeit, through their own actions, some of the expressions of this right to belong, but even then they still belong, and still have a worth which others must not disregard. Segregation whether done by custom or by law is a fundamental contradiction of this basic right. Racial segregation is a glaring example when men and women are excluded from the society of others not on the ground of their behaviour but on the basis of appearance; in practice, the full expression of their humanity is disallowed. It is of course a very different matter when a group chooses to meet to share a common culture, a common religious faith, or common ethical principles and welcomes all who share those beliefs. This is to do with character and convictions and is not on the basis of appearance. So church schools or muslim schools are a proper use of liberty.

All men have a right to share in the earth and its riches, because God has given the earth to them as a whole; they have a right to possess. All that makes for human fulfilment in education, culture, leisure and enjoyment belongs to man 'made in the image of God'. Though capacities and interests vary, no one has an inherent greater or lesser right to share in the resources made available to mankind. It is a flagrant distortion of God's will when unequal opportunity and privilege is given through accidents of birth or appearance. There is a need for deep care and concern for deprived communities, especially the large black communities in urban Britain which are in danger of alienation from British society. There needs to be practical equality of opportunity, and not only theoretical, in the realm of employment, housing and education. There should be among Christians a passionate concern for those who start from a position of disadvantage and deprivation.

The fact that all are made in the image of God does not mean that each individual is identical – far from it. An essential element in being in the image of God is personality, the right to be one's self! The fact that a man's racial, cultural, economic and family group is known, does not predetermine every detail of his behaviour. He is himself and no other. The Christian will be wary of pre-judging individuals, labelling them, stereotyping them, depriving them of their reputation without examining their character and actions. He will work for a human society where individuality is not crushed, where character is valued rather than superficial appearances, and where people seek to understand and to accept each other rather than to condemn and to reject others. Respect for individuals includes respect for their culture, and their convictions.

The attainment of ideals is always difficult and never complete in human society, because man does not now possess his primordial innocence. It is essential that the dimensions of evil are not under-estimated, for the Fall has affected every part of life. Sin and evil are woven into the fabric of society. Fallen humanity is exhibited not only in the criminal, but also in the police, the law-abiding public, the institutions of the state, the language practices and intentions of the law. All this does not mean that there are no differences between men or between cultures. There are better and worse. Some cultures and societies are more just and compassionate than others, but human life operates in the realm of comparatives not absolutes. For while there is an idealistic side even in the worst of men and societies, self-interest is at the root of individual and group behaviour to a great extent. In the behaviour of both individual and group, the New Testament sees not only 'the flesh', but also demonic forces at work, in the mind of the individual (2 Corinthians 4:4), and in the values, customs and life-style of the group (1 John 2:16).

The implications of the extent of evil are very many. Not only does the ideal not now exist, but in this world the ideal is unobtainable. Furthermore, these forces are at work within the Christian community, even though the Holy Spirit is at work to lead and direct in a different direction and toward different goals. Although this is the case, Scripture nowhere gives encouragement to men to abandon the goals and the ideals, and to give way to inertia or despair. While there is in the Bible an attempt to provide limitations on the consequences of human perversity and folly because it exists, there is no abandonment of God's requirements. The state has a significant role in restraining the inhumanities of men, in minimizing the evil consequences of human waywardness, and in redressing injustice; but it is not the sole or the chief instrument for achieving God's will on earth. In the drafting of laws the Christian will want, or ought to want, the ideal provided by God to be kept fully in view, while recognizing the limitations occasioned by sin.

It is, however, all too possible for the proper function of the law in minimizing evil and redressing injustice to become distorted into a reinforcement of injustice; a siding with the sinner rather than the sinned-against. In Scripture, the ideal life-long union of one man and one woman in marriage is maintained, while in the Old Testament divorce was regulated to limit the evil done. This attempt to give a measure of protection to the divorced woman became in the hands of men a new 'ideal', bestowing divine approval on the oppressive conduct of the strong and their treatment of the weak. So it must always be asked: 'Is the expressed intention of the law and its actual operation such as to reduce the evil done to the weak? Or is it in practice simply reinforcing the wrongdoer's actions'? Thus a law against racial discrimination seeking to protect the disadvantaged is acceptable, even though this infringes the human freedom to choose. Any gain from the law is to the oppressed, and any loss of freedom comes from the prejudiced. On the other hand, to write racial discrimination into the law (as for instance in immigration law), whatever the stated intentions, is not acceptable as a concession to human sinfulness, for this adds the weight of the law to the side of the prejudiced, and deprives the sinned-against of their rights.

There are many formidable obstacles in the pursuit of social justice. The challenge for the Christian in facing the racial and cultural diversity in Britain is to put into concrete terms the revolutionary style of life lived by Christ; to translate into economics, education, politics, and human relationships the claim that he is 'a new creation', who looks at no one and no situation from simply a human point of view of self-interest and self-concern. A love for others will result in the Christian being concerned for the total good of others: material, social and spiritual. A concern for the social and material should not be a substitute for man in his relationship with God, nor should it be viewed as a convenient bridge to the spiritual; rather, because he knows God, he reflects the character of God. 'I am the Lord who practises kindness, justice and righteousness in the earth, for in these things I delight' (Jer. 9:24).

RELIGIOUS AND CULTURAL LIBERTY

The majority community inevitably exerts pressure towards conformity on minority communities. It does so by interaction through work, through the media and especially through education. Some attention may be given to the values, beliefs and life-style of the minority (this varies enormously); but the philosophy of education, the structure of the education programme, the interaction with peer-group, the quest for acceptance, the eventual need for employment; all promote assimilation of the minority. The reaction to this in the older members of the minority group is often to seek to preserve their identity and to practise their faith more earnestly. Canon Dick Wootton writes 'without these they are "lost", they are deprived of a proper chance to develop their humanity. The growth of large Asian communities within our midst without roots and without religious and moral beliefs would be to no-one's advantage, and a grave loss to the Asians themselves'. There is often tension between the generations, with many of those educated into the English attitudes to choice and values finding strain in their traditional loyalties to the family, the group and the religion.

What is the Christian's responsibility in such a situation? The biblical teaching about man makes plain that God has given him the precious gift of freedom; and that includes the possibility of the wrong use of freedom; mistaken ideas and an inadequate response to him. Old Testament Israel was a nation chosen by God to be his people, and was commanded by God to enforce true religion and to prohibit false. Modern Britain (or any other nation) is not God's chosen people; the new Israel is the Christian Church. Discipline is proper and necessary within the Church with regard to faith, worship and practice; but outside its boundaries it is not the New Testament function of the state to enforce Christian belief and practice. On the contrary for the state to act in such a way would undermine the nature of the gospel with its stress on the cross of Christ, the power of God to save everyone who believes, and the weakness of God proving to be his strength. The appeal of the apostles was not to secular and political authority : 'The weapons we use in our fight are not the world's weapons, but God's powerful weapons, with which to destroy strongholds. We destroy false arguments; we pull down every proud obstacle that is raised against the knowledge of God; we take every thought captive and make it obey Christ'. (2 Corinthians 10 :4–5)

In modern Britain there are strong pragmatic arguments

against any attempt to use secular authority to bolster the gospel. Religious liberty is a tender plant and can easily be destroyed; evangelical Christians are a small minority and would very soon suffer if it were lost; the state's desire for tranquillity and order are very soon invoked to stop the disturbing consequences of evangelism among those of other beliefs. However, the Christian is called to principled opposition to coercion even when he has the possibility of exerting pressure other than that of the truth of the gospel and the love of Christ. The Christian needs to reject implicit coercion as well as explicit; just allowing a 'Christianizing' process to take its course ought to be more acceptable than direct legal pressure. Thus the desire of some Sikhs to wear turbans at work or on motor cycles is surely part of their religious liberty, and does not significantly affect the rights of others. A Muslim who wishes to leave an assembly-line for prayer is in a different position because of the implications for people of other beliefs or none.

There are two issues which are of special importance : the use of church property, and religious education. In inner-city areas there is a shortage of places that are available for worship and assembly; the church often owns the buildings and sites available for collective activity. The simultaneous use of church property for Christian worship and for the worship of another faith inevitably produces confusion in the minds of people in the locality; practice undermines any verbal statement about the uniqueness of Christ. However, if the Christian commitment to freedom of worship and assembly is to be given positive expression, there needs to be a willingness to consider selling redundant sites and buildings and positively to assist those who wish to find places for worship. It is felt by many Christians that to sell a church to a non-Christian group is an admission of the failure of the gospel; it is plain for all to see that what was once a Christian centre has now been handed over as a mosque or gudwara. It should be no part of a Christian's life, or of church practice, to disguise the reality. If Christians have moved from that area, or if local people have abandoned the worship of

Christ, it is difficult to justify retaining an empty shell; for 'the most high God does not live in houses built by men' (Acts 7:48). In quite a number of areas this issue is largely a thing of the past; groups now seeking buildings can in many cases be splinter groups from existing churches and temples. The principle of freedom of worship and assembly does not of course mean the promotion of fragmentations in religious groups.

The issues involved in Religious Education are much wider than the contents of the syllabus. The contents of the syllabus must of course be decided on educational grounds, not on questions of evangelistic opportunity. It is right that all children should learn something about different faiths. The presence of children from different backgrounds can lead to a very natural growth in understanding and respect. However, there are dangers in the present situation that in the supposed interest of minority religious groups, all religious education will be reduced, or that syncretistic and eclectic faith will be taught, which is true neither to Christianity nor Islam nor Sikhism. The wider issue in education is the question 'To what extent is Englishizing necessarily Christianizing'? A concern for individual liberty, the value of truth, and other 'liberal' virtues are the products of a Christian culture. To what extent are they likely to be rejected by other faiths? Traditional Hinduism does not look at truth, nor does Islam look at liberty in the way that is characteristically English. On the other hand there is no contradiction in being an English Jew, for there is a common cultural background in the Old Testament. Diet, clothing and cultural ideas are bound to be altered through the educational system; it is unrealistic to pretend otherwise. Christians will want to be very sensitive and sympathetic to the tensions produced inside both the older and younger generations.

EVANGELISM AND CHURCH GROWTH

The New Testament Church was culturally, racially and socially mixed. The first row in the Church arose because of the cultural diversity of the Church. In Acts 6, before any Gentiles had become Christians, there was a disagreement between the Greek-speaking and the Aramaic-speaking Jewish Christians; the Greek-speaking Christians complained about discrimination against their widows. The significant thing is that both groups belonged to the one Christian community; there would have been no possibility of argument if they had belonged to two separate bodies. As it is, they were sharing together in very practical ways by sharing their possessions, and using the proceeds to provide for the needy in the Christian community. Tensions arose in the fellowship, following the 'natural' division along the cultural lines. The apostles sought to ensure that there was no discrimination (and there was seen to be no discrimination) in the one Christian Church. The church at Antioch is described in Acts 11:19–20 and 13:1–3. It quite evidently included both Jews and Gentiles, and the leaders were drawn from various backgrounds, 'Simeon, called the black' was a dark-skinned African, Lucius came from Cyrene in North Africa, Barnabas from Cyprus, Manaen had a court background having been educated with Herod. It is difficult to imagine a group that was more diverse than the Christians at Antioch – culturally, racially and socially diverse, yet united in one Christian group. It is quite evident that their oneness was not of a purely 'spiritual' or 'theoretical' variety; they shared life together in sharing in meals in one another's homes. It was the behaviour of Peter and Barnabas in ceasing to eat with Gentiles at Antioch owing to the prejudice of Jewish Christians from Jerusalem that produced Paul's outburst in Galatians 2.

Evangelism and church building were done across cultural, social and racial lines. In the Acts Jews shared the gospel with Gentiles – Peter with Cornelius, Paul with a Philippian gaoler, Philip with the Ethiopian eunuch. It is not surprising that this should be the dominant example of crossing racial, social and cultural barriers in evangelism and church building; Jews became Christians first. However we also see the beginnings of the evangelism of Jews by

Gentiles; in Acts 16 Timothy the son of a Gentile father begins to work with Paul among Jews. It is true that Peter and Paul agreed that Peter should work among the Jews whilst Paul was working among the Gentiles; but that was more a question of the area of working. Paul always went to evangelize Jews as well as Gentiles.

All this was done from deep conviction, and was not just the way things happened. It arose out of the nature of the gospel: 'For you were baptized into union with Christ, and so have taken upon yourselves the qualities of Christ himself. So there is no difference between Jews and Gentiles, between slaves and freemen, men and women, you are all one in union with Christ' (Galatians 3:27–28). Baptism, outwardly with water, inwardly by faith in Christ, was the start of the Christian life. It brought them into the one body of Christ. The cultural and racial difference (Jew and Gentile), the social difference (slaves and freemen), and sexual difference (men and women) no longer separated them. They all belonged to Christ and therefore to each other in one Christian fellowship. In Ephesians 2:11–3:6 Paul explains that God's purpose was to make peace through the death of Christ, peace between men and God and peace between men and men. Over and over again Paul emphasizes the reconciling purpose of God in Christ: 'By his death on the cross Christ destroyed the hatred; by means of the cross he united both races in one single body and brought them back to God' (2:16). It belongs to the very nature of the gospel that the Church is built across cultural, social and racial barriers. There are siren voices, as well as gut reaction, telling Christians that the way to success in evangelism is to follow the natural divisions, and to try to build churches along cultural, social and racial divisions. In doing so they ignore the 'success' in the New Testament in crossing these lines; more importantly they are in fact stressing success more highly than the truth of the gospel. To buy success at the price of treating the fundamental nature of the gospel as dispensable is to follow a false gospel.

In Britain the present situation differs from the New

Testament one in several ways. There was a common language throughout the 'civilized' world of the first century, but this is not always true in Britain. In the New Testament, Greek was spoken throughout the Roman Empire, so the early missionaries did not have to contend with learning different languages as they moved from one part to another. Paul nevertheless gives the principle to be adopted when such a situation is to be faced in 1 Corinthians 14:10. He stresses the importance of people being able to 'understand'. 'Understanding' is of course more than simply having the gospel in your own tongue; language cannot be separated from culture. For true understanding, the gospel must be expressed in the thought-forms and the culture of the listeners. Evangelism and church life in the New Testament reflected the variety of culture, but in Britain this is usually not so. Paul adopted the customs and life-style of the group he was trying to win, yet without compromising the truth of the gospel (1 Corinthians 9:19–22). Race highlights the fact that in our congregational life we usually do not reflect the variety of cultures. There are Asian, West Indian, and Anglo-Saxon congregations worshipping and meeting close to each other. These groups meet at work and in school, but not always in church. If the church is middle class and intellectual in the language of the services, in the music employed, in the life-style expected of Christians, in its leadership, and in the methods of presenting the gospel, then the whole atmosphere is such as to repel those who are not middle class and intellectual. They feel out of place and unwanted, even if they are given a friendly greeting at the door.

The life of the New Testament Church was evidence of the supernatural; God was in their midst. The power of Christ was a reality. The fellowship could not be explained in simple natural terms. A church divided on social and racial lines is not evidence for the supernatural, but for the simply human and social. The existing divisions amongst churches along social and racial lines will not be overcome at all easily. It cannot be right to suggest or imply 'I believe in church unity, you must come and join me'! There are however ways of moving by God's grace towards the ideal such as joining in worship for special services at Christmas and Good Friday, sharing in social events and common evangelistic endeavours and regular meetings of ministers. All are things worth doing, and are ways of expressing our unity in Christ. Groups that are divided by language, culture and history need to explore every avenue for fellowship across the divisions. Otherwise, although we may be more 'comfortable', we shall be missing the challenge and rewards of living the gospel.

If strong multi-racial churches are to develop in urban Britain, then the whole Church in Britain will have to take the issues seriously. The theology of incarnation is fundamental; Jesus came to live among those for whom he died to save. The Christian has always to be identified closely with those to whom he is called to witness. More than physical presence is needed, there needs to be a psychological presence too. It is possible to live in one area whilst having one's children educated outside it, and for one's thought-life and friendships to be in quite a different world. If the presence is to be real it needs to be a committed and involved presence in the local church life, and in the local community. True involvement will exclude paternalistic and patronizing attitudes and will involve a willingness to receive as well as a willingness to share and to give.

At the moment Christians are conspicuous more by their absence than by their presence; they have too readily conformed to the values and aspirations of the wider community, and have left struggling churches to join the stronger suburban church in more congenial surroundings. Is not their Lord calling his people to return to the back streets of our inner-city multi-racial communities to strengthen the weak churches already in existence in these areas? Christian periodicals and preachers in all kinds of areas have a responsibility in educating themselves, and in helping to inform the Christian public as to the missionary needs of Britain. If Christians are to move their homes then they will need spiritual and psychological support in the new and perhaps harsher environments they find themselves in, with continuing interest from the sending church as well as the fellowship of the new local church.

A weak church can very easily turn in on itself, concentrating on staying alive and maintaining the plant, rather than thinking of service. If their presence in the community is to be truly evangelical and Christ-centred, Christians must be known as the loving, serving, helping people of the community, to whom anyone can turn at any time. There are many areas of life where the pattern of the servant Christ needs to be seen and heard, and Christians should seek to discover these and become involved. Service may be through the local church, or through a secular agency or through an Asian community or religious agency. In undertaking any kind of service, there needs to be research as to the real needs of the community, and a genuine listening to the cries and opinions of the different groups in the community. We/they attitudes must be avoided; the co-operation of others, especially in the group needing help, is essential. Among the obvious spheres of service in the secular community are children's playgroups, language teaching amongst Asians, and advice centres. Where these are already existing in the community, Christians should be encouraged to participate with other people of good will in such ventures. Where they do not exist the local church may well be instrumental in creating or stimulating such a response to human need. The ordinary life of the church in neighbourliness and service to people in need ought to be a constant factor over and apart from any special activity. Involvement in Asian cultural activities and community activities may sometimes be difficult because of the religious implications, and also the question of language; nevertheless wherever possible supporting what is good in the community and learning from those of a different cultural background is part of the Christian response.

Dialogue is an essential element in a pluralistic society; as Christians we need to keep open the lines of communication between ourselves and other people. This requires us to learn how to listen to other people; to try to understand their thinking, and their religious beliefs. All this is not easy; it demands patience, understanding and love plus a sensitivity to the gospel. In practice it is often easier, and seems more natural, to start with cultural dialogue, before getting involved in the more personal and controversial religious dialogue. Sharing in the different ways of bringing up children, and the different patterns of marriage, are unthreatening ways of sharing in friendship. Before a Christian group becomes involved in dialogue with those of another faith, it is essential that the group thinks beforehand about its own members' faith and has some basic knowledge of the other faith. Christian groups always contain people of diverse Christian development and understanding. Some, because their faith is somewhat uncertain and unformulated, may become belligerent, hostile and offensive when confronted by someone of another faith. Others, because they do not understand the real differences between the religious faiths, may concede vital Christian truths in order to be friendly. All this underlines the need for thought and care before involvement in dialogue. As well as a firm grasp of Christian essentials, there needs to be a willingness to appreciate what is good in the faith and practice of others. Christians will want to make the point early that their faith and practice is different from British faith and practice. British does not equal Christian. Christians will not wish to give the impression their faith is simply an ethical code like that of many others; they will want to confess the good news of Jesus and that will involve them in sharing his uniqueness.

There are two common failings among Christians. The first is to forget the responsibility of evangelism and witness, and the second is to rush into the preaching of the gospel without the prior requirements of involvement, service and understanding. Neither is the way of Jesus. Our task is to preach Christ crucified, the name above every other name, the saviour and servant of all mankind. Evangelism is clearly a task for all Christians, and the more it can be seen that English, West Indian and Asian Christians are working together in the name of Christ, the more it will be seen that to be a Christian is distinct from being English. The gospel is centred around the person of Jesus, and proclaiming the gospel will involve proclaiming him positively. It is neither wise nor right to spend time attacking the cherished beliefs of others; rather we need positively to commend Christ as the saviour of all men. The difficulties of trying to include different cultural groups in one fellowship are considerable, yet the situation is changing between the generations and if the appeal is made to older cultural forms whether English or Asian then young people will become quickly disenchanted. If there is a real work of the grace and power of God, then the natural cultural barriers can be overcome. The church must not be an oasis of ancient English culture, or the preserve of a particular Anglo-Saxon high-brow intellectual group.

CONCLUSIONS

The vitally important issues which the cultural differences in modern Britain bring to a Christian's attention should be an occasion for rejoicing rather than despondency. There are not just problems in the present situation, but possibilities of enrichment and challenge. The issue of social justice makes plain the need for the Christian to accept the lordship of Christ in every area of life. It is a sharp challenge to relevance. Pluralism in religion and culture provides an opportunity to learn and understand at first hand. It challenges Christians to think afresh about freedom, and the nature of the gospel. With respect to evangelism, missionary work is seen to be the responsibility of many ordinary Christians. It is open to Christians to have a deeper dimension of fellowship than exists between people of like minds and common culture and aspirations. Tensions there will be, but with the grace of God they can prove a deepening and enriching experience.

Questions for discussion

1. What are the positive advantages in belonging to a multi-cultural society?

2. How can we encourage others to see these and to share in them?

3. Examine how much your group or church thinks in terms of we/them. Who are the 'them'? List what you think you know about 'them'. Is this based on 'what everybody knows', the media, or a careful and balanced knowledge? Apply the descriptions to your own group that you have applied to others.

4. What are the implications of believing that 'all are made in the image of God' for education, housing, employment and leisure?

5. 'There should be among Christians a passionate concern for those who start from a position of disadvantage and deprivation'. Why? How should this be expressed?

6. What is the right attitude to church buildings, their use and sale? What light does the New Testament shed?

7. What principles relate to the education of children in a multi-cultural society? Consider all the children as well as those from particular minorities.

8. In your area, is the church life evidence for God at work overcoming social, cultural, racial barriers? Examine the whole 'atmosphere', the leadership, the music, the life-style expected of Christians etc. Where could a start be made in putting right some of the faults?

9. What factors dictate where people live? What different factors should influence Christians? How can Christians be encouraged soberly to live in areas of great human and spiritual need?

10. How can friendships be made so that a genuine sharing of Christ can take place?

6

Global Stewardship[1]

PHILIP KING
General Secretary, South American Missionary Society

Modern technology makes it possible to sit in an armchair in Coventry and watch people starve in Calcutta. Conditioned to becoming passive spectators of suffering we find it difficult to grapple with the soaring statistics of the 'gloom boom'. We switch the channel and hope the problems will go away but they obstinately refuse.

WORLD TRENDS

At the World Council of Churches Assembly at Nairobi in 1975 Professor Charles Birch described the world as being on a 'Titanic course' heading for destruction, the passengers wining and dining, seemingly oblivious to danger. The accompanying chart suggests four factors that override all others – increase of population, poverty, usage of resources and spread of information.

Population

If it continues to increase at the rate of 2% per annum the world's population of 3,700 million will double by the end of the century. Even if the goal of zero population growth were achieved soon after AD 2000 the world population could still increase to the frightening figure of 15,500 million within a century.

This accelerating growth has been compared to a lily which doubles in size every day for thirty days until it fills a pond. Unfortunately, the danger does not loom large until the 28th or 29th day.

The Vicious Spiral

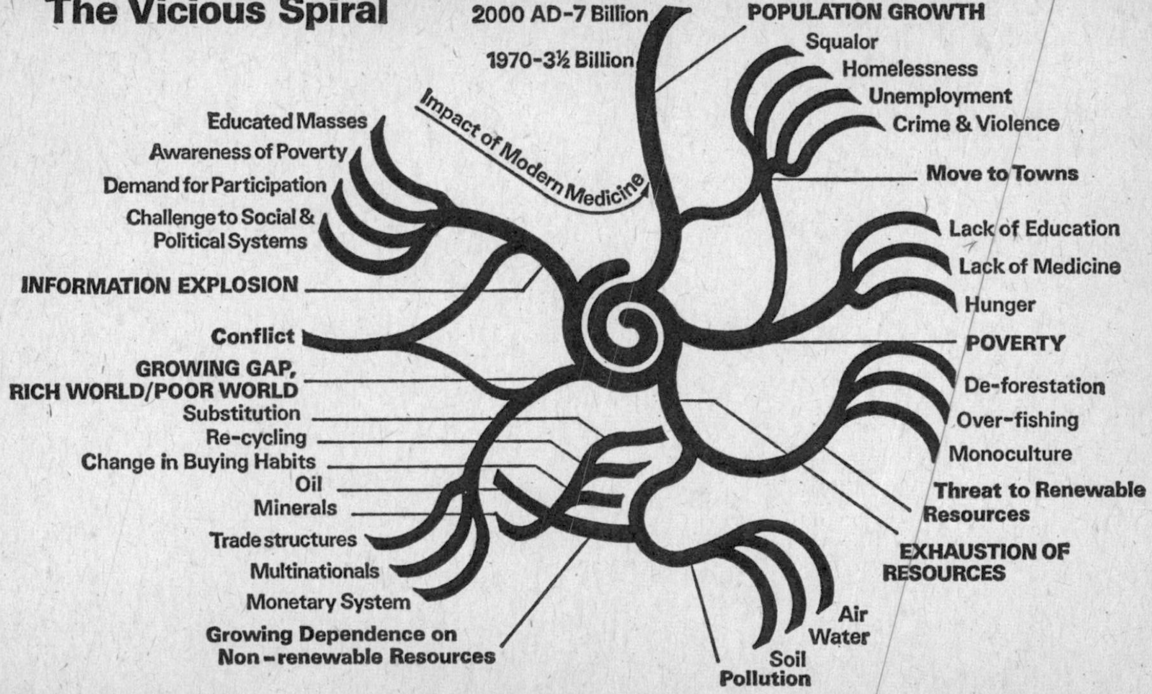

2000 AD–7 Billion
1970–3½ Billion
Impact of Modern Medicine
POPULATION GROWTH
Squalor
Homelessness
Unemployment
Crime & Violence
Move to Towns
Lack of Education
Lack of Medicine
Hunger
POVERTY
De-forestation
Over-fishing
Monoculture
Threat to Renewable Resources
EXHAUSTION OF RESOURCES
Air
Water
Soil
Pollution
Educated Masses
Awareness of Poverty
Demand for Participation
Challenge to Social & Political Systems
INFORMATION EXPLOSION
Conflict
GROWING GAP, RICH WORLD/POOR WORLD
Substitution
Re-cycling
Change in Buying Habits
Oil
Minerals
Trade structures
Multinationals
Monetary System
Growing Dependence on Non-renewable Resources

The population growth rate is highest in the poorer countries. Indeed growth of population and of poverty and malnutrition are reciprocally linked; poor families tend to have large numbers of children and so increase their poverty. Near the top of the league table is India where a century ago over 80% of the population were reasonably well fed; now it is under 2%.[2] Population increase has now stabilized in the UK but we have no reason for complacency. We have a population of 228 per square kilometer (385 in the south east) compared to 164 for India and 22 for the United States. It has been well said that 'over-population is everybody's baby'.

Poverty

Poverty is a vicious circle or spiral involving food, health, shelter, education and political institutions. Malnutrition leads to disease and loss of energy, which in turn affects the ability to work or think. The illiterate cannot decipher instructions for using medicine or agricultural machinery, nor can they read newspapers or gain perspective on issues and thus exercise a reasonable say in affairs. It becomes difficult to provide the needed agriculturalists, doctors and teachers and those that are produced may be unemployable in a country with little economic prosperity.

The world can be broadly divided into the richer 'North', including Russia, Europe, the United States and Canada, and the poorer 'South', including Africa, Asia and Latin America. There are obvious exceptions to this North–South divide such as Australia and South Africa, but in general terms the rich have only 25% of the world's population while generating 90% of its wealth. The average Briton spends more in a month than the average Burmese earns in two years; he spends as much on tobacco as the average Indian spends to keep alive. Furthermore, although output per head is growing in both parts of the world it is growing more slowly in the South, with the exception of countries such as Brazil and Mexico. The gap seems to be widening.

One important feature of the population explosion, apart

from the poverty it generates, is unemployment with the accompanying drift to the city. Lima, the capital of Peru, sucks in 1,000 newcomers every week. The media advertise the luxuries of city life as a modern El Dorado but the peasant arrives to find himself in a poverty trap. The city becomes a 'melting pot' dissolving former traditions and community life, and a 'powder keg' where discontent begins to smoulder. Half the world lives in urban areas and half the Third World urbanites are in slum conditions. By AD 2000 it has been estimated that 90% of the world will be in urban areas. A metropolis may become a megalopolis and later a necropolis.

Resources

The picture is not complete without the warning that certain of the earth's finite resources are being used at an increased pace. One estimate is that if the present rise in consumption continues existing known reserves of petroleum and coal will soon be exhausted.[3] The main factors in this situation are population growth, increased consumption, especially by the developed world, and pollution. 'Civilized Man has marched across the face of the earth and left a desert in his foot prints.'[4] Industrialized nations tend to disturb the life system of our planet by using the air, the rivers and the seas as a dustbin. A single Sunday edition of the New York Times uses 150 acres of forest – 40% of Brazil's forests have been cleared in the last 25 years. Various kinds of mammal are becoming extinct at the rate of one species per year and DDT has so polluted the Baltic that it is dangerous to eat certain fish there regularly.[5]

Information

Information transfer has become a new feature of the world scene. The mass media, tourism, international commerce, the urban drift and primary education give a larger number of mainly poor people an awareness of the growing disparity between themselves and the wealthy of their own and other nations. Expectations are aroused which no political leader is able to fulfil and power in First, Second and Third Worlds is tending to be centralized.

The unequal distribution of power – whether economic or political – is of parallel significance to the unequal distribution of resources. A sense of powerlessness in our increasingly complex world is experienced at the grass roots in rich nations as well as in poor. This has been accentuated by the advent of education programmes and sophisticated methods of communication.

A sense of growing inequality in terms of resources and of power inevitably leads to both criticism and conflict. This is especially so when the ideologies spawning from Marxism can articulate and marshal feelings of resentment. The present nuclear stalemate results in an 'atomizing' of conflict, where different terrorist and guerrilla groups vie with one another; 'having reached agreement that it would make no sense for the world to die of nuclear thrombosis; the world seems to have broken out in a rash of smaller local disputes – each carrying the virus of a general war'.[6] But the great powers have not abdicated; they can manipulate the situation by the sale of arms and watch the conflict from the touchlines. In 1952 the value of the turnover in the international arms trade was 300 million dollars. In 1974 it was 18,000 million dollars.

The need to reverse the vicious spiral of poverty, inequality and conflict becomes increasingly urgent. As President Kennedy put it 'Those who make peaceful revolution impossible make violent revolution inevitable'.

MISSION IN TODAY'S WORLD

To what degree and for what reasons should the Christian be concerned with these world trends? Are they part of our 'mission'? Sometimes 'mission' has been used as an equivalent to evangelism and at other times it has been used to describe everything that God is doing in the world. The best usage lies between these two extremes and covers everything the Church is sent into the world to do; 'As my Father has sent me even so I send you' (John 20:21). The work and ministry of Christ demonstrate a concern that is wider than evangelism. This is why the covenant of the 1974 Lausanne Congress on Evangelism declared that both evangelism and socio-political involvement are part of our Christian duty. Evangelicals must be concerned not only with the Great Commission to make disciples of all nations (Matthew 28:18–20) but also with the Great Commandment to love one another, of which the commission is part (John 15:12). The call to repentance and the new life-style required of the Christian both have socio-political implications as illustrated from the preaching of John the Baptist, Christ's dealings with Zacchaeus and the rich young ruler, the life of the Christian community described in Acts, and the ethical teaching of the epistles. God's purpose is to bring all aspects of human life under the lordship of Christ.[7]

If, however, we restrict the word 'mission' to the activity of God in sending the Church into the world, we must not forget that God is also active in the world outside the Church. His relationship to the world is one of creating, owning, ruling, caring and providing, restraining evil and inspiring good, and directing the course of history. His plan is to sum up all things in Christ (Ephesians 1:10; Colossians 1:20). 'In the sphere of social responsibility our calling is to co-operate with, and even in some measure act as, agents of this common grace which is already at work in unexpected places.'[8]

As Shaftesbury and Wilberforce found, it is very often impossible to demonstrate social concern without political involvement. Those who opt out of such involvement are in practice either advocating a policy of 'laissez-faire' or implicitly justifying the status quo; even this is a political decision. In practice, political guidelines are better established with the help of experts in the pew and not just left to comment from the pulpit though both have their place in promoting a dialogue between theology and other disciplines. The Christian will seek to make objective and constructive criticism of all party programmes, but cannot avoid some party political allegiance in order to achieve specific goals.

It will very rarely be right for the Church as a whole to be identified with one party, though exceptional cases could arise.

It is not so easy to ignore the socio-political dimension of mission in the inner city areas of Britain – still less in the Third World. Samuel Escobar writing from the revolutionary climate of South America quotes a student as saying 'in the past they told us not to worry about changing society because what we need is to change men. New men will change society. But when the new men began to worry about changing society they were told not to worry, that the world has always been bad . . . why try to make it better? What is even worse is that those who teach this are the ones that enjoy all the advantages that this passing world offers'.[9]

The title 'Global Stewardship' can of course apply to the whole of our responsibility for mission and especially to evangelism; we are to be stewards of grace and of the gospel (Ephesians 3 :2–7, 1 Peter 4 :10). This chapter will, however, be devoted primarily to stewardship of the earth's resources, a subject which is increasingly under debate today. This is not to deny the primary importance of evangelism or that the greatest need in the world is the salvation of those who are living and dying without Christ; nor is it to imply that evangelicals do not need fresh motivation or impetus for evangelism. Evangelism is vital not only in its own right but as the secret of achieving a caring and sharing community which is prepared for proper stewardship of resources.

'THE EARTH IS THE LORD'S'

Beginning with the early chapters of Genesis the emphasis of the Bible is that 'the earth is the Lord's' (Leviticus 25 :23; Psalm 24 :1). Although man has been given the responsibility of developing the earth's resources (Genesis 1 :26–28), he does so as steward and not as owner. He is responsible and accountable to God for all that he does (Romans 14 :10–12). Stewardship implies a responsible attitude to nature not so much because of any intrinsic value in nature itself, but because it belongs to the Lord. It also implies a responsibility to our fellow men which we cannot shrug off by claiming that we are not our brother's keeper (Genesis 4:9); this will be developed later.

Western Christianity is often accused of using the mandate to 'be fruitful and multiply and fill the earth' as an excuse for unlimited exploitation of the earth and irresponsible increase in population.[10] However, the problem lies not with the mandate, but with the misuse of it; responsibility and accountability are implied by the phrase – 'Subdue it and have dominion . . .'

Stewardship is to be undertaken against the background of moral precepts summarized in the Ten Commandments. When these are flaunted there results a breakdown of relationships between man and God, his fellows and the created order. There are also physical laws which apply to man's stewardship. Where these are ignored there is a similar breakdown.

From the beginning there may have been elements in nature which required subduing; man's disobedience did not affect his task but his effectiveness. This is illustrated not only from Genesis 3[11] but also from the refusal of Israel to follow instructions on how to treat the promised land; a land flowing with milk and honey became barren, the tree cover disappeared and the soil was eroded away.[12]

Yet where man failed Christ came to restore (Psalm 8; Hebrews 2:5–9, Romans 8:18–25).

Prior to this century when man ignored God's laws and failed to act as a steward with delegated responsibility, the consequences could be contained within nation states. Today the consequences of the actions of one nation, or even of groups of individuals within nations, can have profound consequences elsewhere in the world. Interdependence is now a fact of life. Hence the title 'Global Stewardship'.

HARVEST GROWTH

Discussion on Third World needs often centres on distribution to the exclusion of growth, and 'cutting the cake' is used as a metaphor for sharing resources. It is a misleading one as it suggests something static and unalterable. A more dynamic and biblical metaphor is 'sharing the harvest' – a model which combines the 19th century stress on growth potential with the modern stress on distribution.

There is considerable pressure against an emphasis on growth on the part of those concerned to preserve the earth's resources and to stop the spread of pollution, but these proper concerns relate more to industrial rather than to agricultural development and to the richer North rather than to the South. It is not so much a matter of maximum or zero growth as an optimum growth which will make available the resources to counter pollution and to assist fairer distribution.

Charles Birch's 'Titanic' warning may be over dramatic. 'A Second Look at Doom' by Lord Ashby of Brandon[13] criticizes the earlier doom forecasts by the Club of Rome[14] as being too pessimistic. He points out that yields of wheat in the USA, for instance, increased by 120% in a nineteen-year period from 1954 to 1973.[15] The International Research Centres on rice, potato, maize, wheat and other crops have significant potentials for both South and North in discovering new strains and pioneering new methods. Professor Beckerman likewise criticizes the pollution hysteria by arguing, for example, that even if the whole of the annual production of the world's mercury mines were dumped straight into the sea it would take between 2,500 and 10,000 years before the sea's natural concentration of mercury was doubled. The percentage of grossly polluted rivers in Britain has fallen from 6.4% in 1958 to 3.7% in 1972 and should be 1% in 1980. He predicts that population growth rates will tend to decline by 1980, slowly at first and then rapidly. In calculating reserves of non-renewable resources a distinction must be drawn between known reserves and actual reserves. In 1945 estimated known copper reserves were 100 million metric tons. During the following 25 years 93 million metric tons were mined but present known reserves are over 300 million tons.[16]

Most countries in the Third World have a potential for

growth implied by the word 'developing'. Only 10% of the world's total land surface is used for arable farming and it is possible that another 30% could be brought under cultivation. 75% of the world's surface is water but so far only 1% of the world's food is taken from the sea. It is impossible to predict accurately sources of energy and protein that may be discovered or adapted in future years, especially under the pressure of increasing shortage and rising prices. While the rich need to hear the call to care for the environment and concern for distribution, it is also important to recognize that 'all predictions are unreliable, especially those about the future'. Already recent predictions about the population growth in the United Kingdom have had to be revised as the population has stabilized.

The debate continues. Meanwhile the Christian's attitude must be one of balanced realism – recognizing man's potential for good in the image of God and yet his potential for evil as a fallen sinner. He sees the world as a cockpit for the battle between evil and good, with God as supreme, active in bringing both blessing and judgement.

While over-optimism would be unrealistic and dangerous, it would be equally fatal to become mesmerized into giving up hope of a considerable increase in harvest growth. This is, after all, our first responsibility as stewards of God's earth. There is no hint in Scripture that the resources available will be inadequate for responsible stewardship. The covenant promise to Noah and all mankind is that seedtime and harvest will not fail (Genesis 8:20–9:11). Even today there is enough protein in the world for both current and predicted needs. In spite of man's disobedience God has not abdicated from his providential ordering of the world – sustaining, upholding, governing and restraining.

The covenant with Noah and its promise of continuing resources, however, needs to be balanced by the warnings of judgement leading up to the end of time. The crucible of man's future includes wars, disasters and famine, with judgement on any affluent society which reduces men to commercial bondage (Revelation 18), but the goal is a new megalopolis, where God's glory is paramount (Revelation 21 and 22).

HARVEST SHARING AND HARVEST MANAGEMENT

As suggested above, man has a responsibility to God as his steward for responsible development of the earth's resources. He also has a responsibility to God and to his fellow men for just distribution of these resources. But what is the basis of 'justice' in sharing the harvest? Justice is nowadays linked with the idea of equality. This is a far cry from the Victorian approach – 'the rich man in his castle, the poor man at his gate, God made them high and lowly, and ordered their estate'. Neither extreme gives the Christian balance. Equality on its own is an inadequate concept; too often it is only achieved at the cost of losing identity, variety and freedom. Furthermore, individuals clearly differ in their possession of natural endowment and countries in their natural resources. Emil Brunner argues that man, created in the image of God, has both an essential dignity and equality, and yet an inequality of gifts and duties. His essential equality is not inconsistent with or necessarily destroyed by the hierarchies of family and society.[17] A parallel might be drawn with the essential equality and yet the subordination of function in the persons of the Trinity. Bishop John Taylor suggests 'equipoise' as an alternative to equality in the sphere of distributive justice. The ideal is a 'readiness to fit one's own need to the needs of others and to submit self-assertion to the claims of an equipoise society'. The essential fault is one of disproportion rather than of inequality.[18] Donald Hay declares that every person needs a minimum standard of food, clothing and housing to maintain a human existence and dignity[19], but there is also a maximum limit.

If we follow this analysis, the condemnation of Dives in his treatment of Lazarus was on the grounds of disproportion rather than of inequality. Likewise Amos condemned not wealth as such but disproportionate luxury in the context of others' needs (Ch. 3:13–4:1; 6:4; 6:6).

One of the biggest barriers to increased growth and fair distribution is 'bad management'. There are privileged groups within developing countries who manage the economy for the benefit of themselves and not for the nation as a whole. In the North there are privileged groups who are in a position to influence international trade terms for the benefit of themselves rather than for the world as a whole. Some Northern spokesmen for the South speak as if greed, hatred and selfishness are to be found only in the North. They are, of course, found in both areas. We shall look first at the situation inside developing countries, then at international aid and trade terms and finally at the argument for international institutions. The issue is one of management and of power. In order to ensure fair distribution of the harvest there needs to be a fair distribution of power.

Developing Countries

Some of the efforts at helping the South have been frustrated for reasons of morality, religion, politics, culture, inappropriate technology, or social structures. Where there is corruption aid may find its way to the wrong pockets, though the recent history of the CIA and of some multinational companies reminds us that this is not limited to the South. Sir Frederick Catherwood has argued that Protestant Christianity seems to produce considerable motivation for economic development[20], whereas some of the tenets of non-Christian religions can be a hindrance. Examples in India are the caste system and the preservation of diseased and unproductive sacred cows.

Political objectives in developing countries, often those of individual leaders, may militate against the long-term interest of the nation. Sometimes development is geared more for defence or national prestige than for feeding the hungry. It is part of Asian culture that rice should be the staple diet, but food deficiency would be significantly alleviated if grain or other rich protein goods were substituted as the main crop wherever possible.

Mistakes have been made in the past by introducing

highly sophisticated western-style technology to many developing countries. As unemployment is usually a major problem, developing projects need to be 'labour intensive', otherwise machines will replace manpower, the wealth in the hands of a few will increase, and a larger number will remain unemployed and have no resources to buy the goods produced.[21] It was originally thought that the South could follow the North's pattern of development and that industrialization would automatically spread from the centre outwards. But in fact industrial centres in developing countries are too often enclaves of modernization sucking in the unemployed from rural areas, creating vast shanty towns and increasing the disparity between the rich few and the poor multitudes. Jawarharlal said of India 'We have atomic energy and we also use cow dung'.[22]

Social structures in developing countries can also be a barrier to development where land and wealth are in the hands of the minority – as in much of Latin America and the Middle East. Economic expansion can bring great wealth to the plutocracy without proportionate benefit to the poor. This has been the case in recent years in Brazil. In these cases it may be right to make reform of social structures a condition for giving aid, especially where there is also repression and denial of human rights.

Developed Countries

We turn now from the South to the North. Greed and selfishness affect the nations of the North both in their internal structures and their external relationships, but for the purpose of this discussion we will deal with only the latter. The economic effects of the colonial era vary from country to country and are hotly debated. Some argue that many nations in the South would not now be developing at all had it not been for colonialism; others that economic development tended to take place in enclaves and brought greater economic benefits to the North. The critics of the North claim that geographic colonialism has given way to economic colonialism, and United States business operations in Latin America are cited as evidence. For example, the United Fruit Company is said to control over 50% of the foreign earnings, and therefore a significant proportion of the economic life, of six Latin American countries.

Multi-national companies have come in for a good deal of criticism. At their best they can bring three positive benefits to developing countries – finance, expertise and management. These are used to develop natural resources, train nationals, find new markets for the products, and provide new technological expertise. At their worst they can sometimes result in a wealth and brain 'drain' and have too great an influence on the economic and political life of a country. It may be very difficult for the government of a developing country acting on its own to have adequate checks on their activities.

A good deal of aid has been given by governments of the North to governments of the South, but it has often had ideological or economic strings attached. Between 1945 and 1960 the United States gave three times the aid to Nationalist China (Taiwan) than it gave to the vast continent of neutral India; its aid has often been used in Latin America to bolster repressive regimes against communist influence. Economic influence therefore has sometimes been used to replace the cruder weapon of military intervention. Fanon accused the United States of saying to Cuba 'Since you want independence, take it and starve'.[23] Even where aid has been free of ideological strings it has not always been free of economic advantage to the giver. While it is understandable that few countries will want to give aid to those whose ideologies oppose their own, it is difficult to defend a situation where aid becomes a bribe for another's allegiance. 90% of aid at the moment is bilateral, often creating for the receiving country a humiliating dependence on the donor. The wrong kind of aid can lead to a vicious circle of inflation, balance of payment difficulties, more appeals for aid and thus more dependence on foreign assistance. Pierre Mousa has said 'The young and poor nations are in danger of entering the stage of history with the mental paraphernalia of the prostitute, and the big powers are to blame'.[24] The dignity of the individual, whether in isolation or grouped as a nation, suggests that wherever possible aid should be multi-lateral; channelled through an international agency to those who need it.

One of the factors in harvest management which has caused a sense of injustice is that the North tends to provide shipping and finance. At the same time some northern nations use tariffs and quotas to protect their economy at the expense of the South. (A tariff is the tax levied on imports at the port of entry, and a quota restricts the amount which can enter.) The prices of many primary products from the South – such as tea, copper and cotton – have not kept pace with inflation, while the cost of importing industrial goods has risen dramatically. Ten years ago, Ghana could buy a tractor from overseas by exporting one ton of cocoa; today she has to export about five tons.

Inevitably Christians differ in emphasis on how best to meet the economic needs of the South, a difference which is affected in part by basic political presuppositions. Some emphasize the need for more aid, some the need to give developing countries better opportunities and terms for trade, and some argue for a radical change of structures at all levels – those of international trade and finance as well as political and economic structures within both developed and developing countries. At one end of the spectrum are those who feel that the dangers of a capitalist system are most clearly revealed in the economic relationships between the North and the South and would compare the giving of aid without radical change in structures to the setting up of a first aid post outside the gates of a factory in order to treat workers injured by dangerous machinery inside. What is needed, they would argue, is modification or replacement of the machinery. According to this line of argument some forms of aid may give short-term help but cause long-term harm by bolstering the status quo and so releasing some of the pressure for revolutionary change.

Without necessarily taking our stand at this end of the

spectrum we could argue that some modifications to existing trade rules are needed in order to ensure international co-operation and control, while leaving room for initiative and enterprise.

International co-operation

The task of harvest management is one needing international co-operation, and one of the greatest hindrances to such co-operation is a narrow nationalism which sees no further than national frontiers. The arguments for a welfare state are arguments for a welfare world but too often our socialism (and conservatism) stops at Dover. This is not to deny the value and importance of national and local loyalties, but Christians who have a universal religion should take a lead in reminding each nation of its global responsibilities. Mankind is one, created in the image of God, prior to division into nations. God created one world and provides for one world. The cross breaks down the dividing wall of nationality, and new life in Christ means the creation of a 'single new humanity', without, of course destroying all that is good in cultural identity (Ephesians 2 : 14–15). The Church is called to preach this gospel to the whole world, and the final goal is a congregation of all races and nations united in the worship of God (Revelation 7 :9–10). The reference in St Paul's Athens sermon to God's making of nations and determination of boundaries (Acts 17 :26) cannot, in the light of Old Testament and other history, mean the preservation for all time of national boundaries or separate identity; in the same verse Paul speaks of allotted periods of time; its meaning must be simply that God is Lord of history.

It is difficult to ensure international co-operation without the authority of international law and international institutions. International law has value as a record of international agreement and is a tool for moral persuasion; but without effective international institutions to define, apply and enforce it, its value is limited. It is created largely by treaty and too often promises like pie crusts are made to be broken.

The United Nations is the forum for much debate and occasional action. In the sphere of North/South relations the United Nations Conference on Trade and Development (UNCTAD) is the most significant institution, though it has little executive power. The fourth UNCTAD conference at Nairobi in 1976 demonstrated the conflict brought about by the different analysis of the economic relations that exist between the developed and the developing world.

Clearly it will not be possible to ensure larger harvest growth and fairer sharing of it without greater sharing of decisions in harvest management. It has been argued that man's essential dignity and equality call for some participation in decision-making within a nation's industry.[25] The same principle suggests greater participation by the nations of the South in determining the patterns and rules of international trade.

THE PARTNERSHIP PRINCIPLE

The fact that all men are created in the image of God suggests not only an essential dignity and equality but also a capacity for the exercise of rational choice. This must have relevance for relationships between nations as well as for relationships between individuals. It is on these grounds that one can argue against forms of aid that create a humiliating dependence, and for the development of indigenous leadership and for greater participation by the nations of the South in determining the patterns and rules of international trade. The principle is partnership – a middle way between paternalism, where programmes are dictated in London, New York or Brussels, and orphanism where the needy are deserted altogether.

The principle is easier to formulate than to practise. There are sound reasons why agencies should formulate criteria, build up an expertise for development and try to ensure that limited funds are not wasted, especially where there may be a risk of mismanagement. But it may not always be easy to do this without giving an impression of paternalism, and there may be occasions when groups in receiving countries must be allowed to learn by mistakes. Wherever there are strict criteria, receiving governments, churches and other groups have to shape their programme to fit them; this is so even when dioceses and local churches prefer attractive 'projects' to the making of 'block grants'. The dividing line between partnership and paternalism is not easy to draw.

Mao Tse Tung had a helpful description of the interplay between the theories of the expert and the practice of grassroots experience. 'Go to the practical people and learn from them; then synthesize their experience into principles and theories; and then return to the practical people and call upon them to put these principles and methods into practice so as to solve their problems and achieve freedom and happiness'.[26]

International partnership in the gospel is a frequent theme in the New Testament (e.g. Philippians, especially 1:5; 4:14–19). In order to stimulate the development of indigenous leadership, foreign personnel will need to adopt a servant role from the first. There may be occasions when it is right to withdraw altogether for a time to allow leadership to develop, but the norm for an interdependent (1 Corinthians 12) international community is to seek for a continuing foreign presence, provided that this principle is applied to the North as well. We need the added perspective of enabling Christians of other lands to have a ministry to northern nations, bringing the challenge of their biblical insights, life-style and modes of worship, fellowship and evangelism, to our 'dead bones'.

CHRISTIAN RESPONSIBILITY

If we are to be concerned and involved in socio-political issues on a global scale we shall need to renounce our mental monasticism, to become better informed and to grapple with the issues both individually and in study groups. We must not be afraid of getting our principles muddied in the dirt of politics. For example, the population problem can be tackled by voluntary limitation on the size of families, but what of suggestions of voluntary and compulsory sterilization, or of adding sterilants to the public water supply so as to reduce general fertility levels? The dissemination of biblically consistent ideas and the promotion of debate are urgent. The Christian should also have a significant contribution in identifying the aims of development– whether it should be geared primarily for the increase of production or for the development of man in his dignity, equality and community. Realism about the nature of man will prevent the Christian both from falling into complete despair and from promising a romantic Utopia. Solutions will need to include political ones, reckoning with the facts of power, but bearing in mind the basic principles of justice and freedom.

The need for changes in social structures and trade rules, and the fact that governments have such vast resources at their disposal, and can use power in increasingly arbitrary ways, mean that it is essential for Christians to form pressure groups in order to draw attention to abuse and injustice, and to influence national and international policy. In 1975 for instance, Britain spent about £3,500 million in defence, £6,300 million on alcohol and tobacco, but only £750 million on overseas aid. Fundamental changes in the terms of international trade will inevitably have far-reaching effects in Britain, not least in the field of employment. There may well arise economic arguments similar to those used against Christians who worked for the abolition of slavery. They must be answered in moral as well as economic terms. We have heard before the call for Christians to become involved in trade unions and management and in local and national government. We need to become similarly involved in international consultations and institutions as a vocation, in order to bring Christian principles to bear on policy formulation at this level.

Major educational programmes are also needed to inform voters as well as politicians.

Clearly churches and individual Christians will not be effective in bringing pressure on others unless we can demonstrate our concern by readily sharing our resources. In one sense love is indiscriminate – seeking to meet need wherever it is found and in the form determined by the need. On the other hand, practical love needs a strategy in order to maximize its effectiveness, and the Church's best strategy is to operate through people. The Church's financial resources, apart from use on education and pressure groups, are best channelled through people to people. National workers and foreign personnel can be channels of the love of Christ in evangelism, leadership training, economic and social concern.

If love can be made more effective through a consistent strategy we need to recognize that in a society where freedom of choice is paramount, disaster appeals, long-term development, church planting and leadership training will attract different degrees of support. Thus there is a danger that the shape of our mission may be determined by interest appeal rather than by strategic priority. We need also to remember that considerable secular resources are available for development but not for evangelism; we may therefore need to strike the balance in the opposite direction in our allocation of church funds. A recent Anglican conference in Central Africa pleaded 'the pressures towards physical and economic development in a young country are intense, sometimes at the expense of spiritual values. We ask our partners to remember that, while the World Bank and secular agencies are concerned about poverty, ignorance and disease, it is only to our fellow Anglicans that we can look for the means to provide Christian leaders of integrity for the new Africa'. The millions thronging the cities of the Third World present an urgent need, not only for socio-economic relief but also for evangelism, church planting and teaching. The urban melting pot where age-old traditions are dissolved creates a climate of openness to new ideas, but there is more than one ideology that can fill that vacuum, and the race is on. Bishop Mortimer Arias of Bolivia reminded the 1975 World Council of Churches Assembly in Nairobi of the 2,700 million unevangelized in the world. John Stott, commenting, said 'For many people the quest for justice, liberation, humanization and quality of life are paramount. These concerns are absolutely right, but they should embrace evangelism also. For if justice means the securing of people's rights, is it not their fundamental right to hear the gospel? Is any liberation more radical than freedom from guilt, self and fear by Jesus Christ? Is anything more humanizing than the gospel?'[27]

Evangelism is essential in its own right, but it is also God's method of bringing about that change of heart which motivates us to responsible stewardship of the earth's resources. An agriculturalist working among a primitive Indian community in Northern Argentina declared recently '90% of our problems are human and spiritual ones'. In that particular area the establishment of a Christian church after years of faithful evangelism has made possible an attitude of mutual trust and co-operation essential to the development of a social programme. This is not to say, however, that our socio-political involvement must always be limited to an evangelistic context or to Christian partners.

We also need to consider what are the most appropriate structures to enable effective partnership in mission. When do such structures need to be specifically evangelical or Anglican or both? In the case of relief or development there are fellow travellers on the same road and we may not always want to walk on the other side. Is it wise to divorce the physical and spiritual aspects of mission by setting up separate agencies? Is the voluntary society still the most effective channel for partnership in mission? And if we argue that the official church should be the channel, do we mean the central office, the local congregation or what? How can structures for mission have an international quality, and where is the power base to be located? What should be the Christian's life-style in the light of world needs? Bishop John Taylor suggests a cheerful revolution, using public transport, eating natural foods, resisting the adman's pressures and so on. Whether eating less beef will mean that the protein now used for animal feeding will revert to those who are under-nourished or become cheaper is more open to question. Worldwide, national and local churches need to ask parallel questions. It has been suggested that companies should do a social audit as well as a financial one in order to check on the social effects of their operations. Churches need to do a global audit, whether in planning expensive international conferences or in other operations. The local congregation's expensive new coffee lounge may be essential for its mission in the locality; it is hypocritical for church members living in affluent homes to justify shabby church premises on the grounds of global needs. Yet it is again a matter of proportion; an impression of affluence may not provide an obvious link with the Carpenter of Galilee, especially if the congregation concerned feels unable to increase or even maintain its global giving. It may even find itself indulging in a dual standard of stewardship, saying to the church member 'Obey Christ by giving sacrificially to us and he will supply your needs,' but to the world outside 'We are sorry but times are difficult; we cannot afford any more'.

Certainly the shape of the Church's life-style must be determined not only by world needs; it must be determined by its calling and purpose.

God's plan for the world is to unite all things in Christ, bringing man into proper relationship with himself, to his fellowmen and to the created order. In order to achieve this Christ has been exalted to a supreme position of authority, a position which he holds for the Church. The Church is his body, God's agent to achieve, his laboratory to work out and his showcase to demonstrate this plan (Ephesians 1:9–10; 1:19–23; 2:13–3:11).

To this picture we can add Christ's metaphor of being 'the salt of the earth' (Matthew 5:13). The Church is to penetrate the world without losing its quality or identity in order to prevent the spread of corruption, to heal what is wrong and to bring out the flavour of the goodness of life due to common grace. It is designed to be an international community with every member interdependent (1 Corinthians 12), where power is shared (Ephesians 4:10–16) and where leadership involves sacrifice and service (2 Corinthians 4:5–12; Mark 10:42–45). The focal point of its worship and life involves such a sharing of spiritual and material resources that those who participate without forsaking their selfish habits come into judgement (1 Corinthians 11:20–29; Acts 4:32–5:5). A black South African asked the pertinent question at Nairobi, 'How is it possible for me to share the cup of the Lord's blood with someone whom I know denies me the chance to share a cup of coffee?' The same question might be asked concerning someone who denies the right to a fair price for the same coffee.

As the Church follows this life-style, so its message will be credible and it will begin to fulfil its purpose, becoming a compelling model for international society, and one where global stewardship is normal not exceptional.

Questions for Discussion

1. How far is the idea of equality an adequate basis for the just distribution of power and of resources?
2. How far should and can paternalism be avoided in aid, education and development?
3. What are the values and limitations of patriotism and nationalism?
4. How far should the needs of our own country be put before the needs of others?
5. How can international co-operation be achieved without totalitarianism?
6. What action should be taken to safeguard human rights in the UK and elsewhere?
7. How can Christian debate on world issues be more informed and effective?
8. What difference should a stewardship approach to world resources make on the life-style of the individual Christian, the local church, and the Church at large?
9. How far should it be a Christian priority to mobilize

public opinion and influence governments to tackle global problems in a just way, and how can it be done?

10. What Christian structures would be best suited to promote an international sharing of spiritual and material resources?

NOTES

1. I would like to acknowledge the help given to me in the writing of this chapter by the research group which worked on this topic.
2. *One World One Task*, p. 169.
3. *The Limits of Growth*, Earth Island Ltd, 1972.
4. E. F. Schumacher, *Small is Beautiful*, Abacus, 1974, p. 84.
5. H. Montefiore, *The Question Mark*, Collins, 1969, pp. 21–29.
6. Assistant Secretary of State, Harland Cleveland, 27th February, 1964, quoted in *Nations and Men*, 1966, p. 371.
7. *Let the Earth Hear His Voice*, 1975, Section 5, pp. 65–78, 116–146, and also John Stott, *Christian Mission in the Modern World*, Falcon, 1975, pp. 11–34.
8. J. N. D. Anderson, *Into the World*, Falcon, p. 103.
9. *Is Revolution Change?* IVP, p. 84.
10. Quoted in Paul and Anne Ehrlich, *Population, Resources, Environment*, San Francisco, 1972, p. 359. See also F. Schaeffer, *Pollution and the Death of Man*, Hodder, 1970.
11. Derek Kidner's remarks on Genesis 3:17f, in the Tyndale Commentary of Genesis.
12. *Ecology and Ethics*, IVP, 1972, p. 21.
13. p. 3f.
14. *The Limits of Growth*.
15. p. 3.
16. *In Defence of Economic Growth*, pp. 118, 124, 220 and 237.
17. E. Brunner, *On Justice*.
18. J. V. Taylor, *Enough is Enough*, London, 1975, pp. 44, 45, 49.
19. Donald Hay, *A Christian Critique of Capitalism*, Grove Books, 1975, p. 8.
20. F. Catherwood, *A Better Way*, IVP, 1976, pp. 108f.
21. Schumacher *op cit*, especially p. 143f.
22. Quoted in G. Myrdal, *The Challenge of World Poverty*, Allen Lane, 1974, p. 43.
23. F. Fanon, *The Wretched of the Earth*, McGibbon and Kee, 1965, p. 77.
24. Quoted in J. Hill, *The Disinherited*, Benn, 1970, p. 148.
25. Quoted by Schumacher *op cit*, p. 211.

26. F. Catherwood, *op cit,* pp. 119f.

27. Bulletin of the Evangelical Fellowship in the Anglican Communion, London, March 1976, p. 3.

Also available in Fountain Books

Something Beautiful for God

MALCOLM MUGGERIDGE

'For me, Mother Teresa of Calcutta embodies Christian love in action. Her face shines with the love of Christ on which her whole life is centred. *Something Beautiful for God* is about her and the religious order she has instituted.' *Malcolm Muggeridge*

Instrument of Thy Peace

ALAN PATON

'Worthy of a permanent place on the short shelf of enduring classics of the life of the Spirit.'

Henry P. van Dusen, Union Theological Seminary

Sing a New Song

THE PSALMS IN TODAY'S ENGLISH VERSION

These religious poems are of many kinds: there are hymns of praise and worship of God; prayers for help, protection, and salvation; pleas for forgiveness; songs of thanksgiving for God's blessings; and petitions for the punishment of enemies. This translation of the *Psalms in Today's English Version* has the same freshness and clarity of language, the same accuracy of scholarship based on the very best originals available as *Good News for Modern Man* and *The New Testament in Today's English Version.*

The Gospel According to Peanuts

ROBERT L. SHORT

This book has made a lasting appeal to people of all denominations and none. It has been read and enjoyed by literally millions of people. A wonderfully imaginative experiment in Christian communication.